This book is to be returned on
or before the date stamped below

DEPARTMENT OF THE ENVIRONMENT
CENTRAL UNIT ON ENVIRONMENTAL POLLUTION

POLLUTION CONTROL IN GREAT BRITAIN: HOW IT WORKS

A review of legislative and administrative procedures

Pollution Paper No. 9

LONDON
HER MAJESTY'S STATIONERY OFFICE

This is one of a series of official papers to be published on various aspects of pollution.

Titles already published are:

1. The Monitoring of the Environment in the United Kingdom
2. Lead in the Environment and its Significance to Man
3. The Non-Agricultural Uses of Pesticides in Great Britain
4. Controlling Pollution
5. Chlorofluorocarbons and their Effect on Stratospheric Ozone
6. The Separation of Oil from Water for North Sea Oil Operations
7. Effects of Airborne Sulphur Compounds on Forests and Freshwaters
8. Accidental Oil Pollution of the Sea

FOREWORD

by the Secretary of State for the Environment

In this country both Government and people have long been concerned with the need to control the harmful effects of the wastes which arise from many of man's activities. These wastes take many forms and pose many problems.

They have arisen, or have been identified as important, at various stages of our economic and social development. All this is reflected in the variety of measures and arrangements which have been, and still are being, developed to deal with them.

It is, I believe, of great importance to understand how this complex system operates. Accordingly this report outlines the current legislative and administrative arrangements for pollution control in Great Britain.

I hope that it will provide a valuable guide for the many people in this country concerned with or interested in the protection of our environment from pollution. And that, in addition, it will help those abroad who are concerned to understand the operation of pollution control here.

PETER SHORE

Secretary of State for the Environment

CONTENTS

The factual information given in this booklet has been as far as possible corrected up to August 1976.

CHAPTER 1

INTRODUCTION

1. Great Britain has a long history of concern about the protection of the environment, dating back to the reforms of the great Victorian administrators, whose awareness of the need to protect public health saw the creation of such legislation as the first Alkali Act of 1863, controlling the emission of noxious gases from alkali works, and the 1848 Public Health Act which led to improvements in the water and sewerage services. The machinery of pollution control has developed over the years in response to new environmental hazards and to increased scientific awareness of their implications, and because of public and governmental concern at the potential effects on human health of various pollutants. In consequence we are now at a comparatively advanced stage in the development and adoption of environmental protection policies. This booklet attempts to provide a guide to the controls which exist and the competent authorities for exercising those controls in different fields, and to list selections of the available literature dealing with the allocation of responsibilities in the area of pollution control. Details of all publications cited in the booklet are given in the bibliography.

2. At central Government level most pollution problems are dealt with by the Department of the Environment (DOE) in conjunction as appropriate with the Scottish and Welsh Offices. DOE is concerned with air and fresh-water pollution, noise pollution other than from aircraft, the disposal of solid and radioactive wastes, and oil and chemicals on beaches in England and Wales. Other Departments are, however, involved. The control of marine pollution by oil and pollution (including noise and emissions) from civil aviation activities lies with the Department of Trade (DT); and the Ministry of Agriculture, Fisheries and Food (MAFF) in England and Wales and the Department of Agriculture and Fisheries for Scotland (DAFS) have responsibility through the Pesticides Safety Precautions Scheme for the safe use of agricultural pesticides. MAFF and DAFS also seek to protect our fisheries, both freshwater and at sea, and in relation to this control marine pollution and dumping at sea. The Health and Safety Commission has certain responsibilities for pollution control as part of its general purpose of securing the health and safety of persons both at work or affected by work activities, and of controlling certain emissions into the atmosphere. The Department of Health and Social Security (DHSS) and the Scottish Home and Health Department (SHHD) provide advice for other Government Departments on the health hazards posed by pollutants (see Annex A).

3. Since several Government Departments are involved in the development of policies for the control of pollutants, co-ordination is needed between sectors

1

to ensure that control exercised in one sphere does not act to the detriment of another part of the environment and that an overall view is taken of priorities. The Secretary of State for the Environment has the general responsibility of co-ordinating the work of the Government on environmental pollution, and in this he is assisted by the directorates forming the Environmental Protection and Water Engineering command within DOE, of which the Central Unit on Environmental Pollution (CUEP) is one. The Unit is required to conduct across-the-board appraisals of pollution problems; to provide the central management capability for an overall monitoring and assessment system for the United Kingdom, including co-ordination of the work of the monitoring management groups referred to in paragraph 12; to maintain contact with various specialist groups within and outside Government that are concerned with pollution; to ensure as far as possible that potential problems are not overlooked; and to see that the United Kingdom contributions to European and International Environment protection programmes are properly organised. The Secretaries of State for Wales, Scotland and Northern Ireland are responsible for overall pollution control co-ordination in their respective countries.

4. Some arrangements for pollution control in Scotland and Wales differ from those in England and are shown separately in the following chapters. Throughout the booklet reference to "the Secretary of State" should be taken as meaning the Secretaries of State for the Environment, Wales and Scotland, unless otherwise specified. Pollution control arrangements in Northern Ireland are not covered in this publication, but information may be obtained from the Northern Ireland Office.

5. Because the effects of pollution are usually experienced first within the confines of particular localities, one of the principles followed by successive Governments has been that the primary responsibility for dealing with pollution problems should rest as far as is practicable with authorities operating at a local or regional level, principally local authorities and the water authorities. Thus central Government lays down the statutory framework for pollution control, but implementation is delegated to a large extent to local level. Authorities may in many areas exercise a considerable degree of discretion as to the limit they impose on the release of local pollutants, so that account may be taken of local resources and social priorities, the uses to which surrounding areas are put and the capacity of the environment to absorb pollutants.

6. The most recent legislation in this sphere, exemplifying the application of this principle, was the 1974 Control of Pollution Act, parts of which have now been implemented. The Act extends a wide range of new powers to local and water authorities. It affects almost all aspects of pollution control, amending existing legislation where this has become out-dated in the light of changed conditions and tackling problems for which comprehensive legislation has not previously existed at all. It has increased the powers of the relevant authorities to deal with air pollution and noise and will also increase their powers to deal

with solid wastes and water pollution. Details of the implementation of the Act are given in Annex B.

7. Central Government does, however, retain control of certain pollution problems. On national issues central Government issues guidance, advice and requests to the responsible local or regional authorities. In a limited number of cases national standards are set—e.g. for exposure to radio-active materials; for polluting products that have a more than local effect because they are sold or transmitted throughout the country or move from place to place, e.g. polluting emissions or noise from motor vehicles; or for some air-borne pollutants. Controls for these types of pollutants are generally exercised by central Government or national agencies.

8. Apart from these national standards, most of which relate to products,* there is no general equivalent in United Kingdom legislation to the detailed and uniform environmental standards, either for particular emissions or for general environmental quality, enshrined in the legislation of many other industrial countries. Authorities, both central and local, are expected to operate on the philosophy that standards should be reasonably practicable (in the case of the Alkali Inspectorate and HM Industrial Pollution Inspectorate the best practicable). This philosophy involves the use and maintenance of equipment and the operation and supervision of processes in such a way as to ensure that any discharges, effluents or wastes are controlled as far as is practicable, having regard among other things to local conditions and circumstances, to the current state of scientific and technical knowledge and medical knowledge of the potential harm or nuisance involved, and to the financial implications. This pragmatic approach permits the establishment of individual standards for polluting emissions from particular factories which can be made continually more stringent in the light of technical advance and of changing environmental needs, but allows greater flexibility than statutory standards.

9. Great Britain also adheres to the principle that the "polluter pays", i.e. that the person or organisation creating the pollution should be financially responsible for controlling it. No specific grants are given towards pollution control equipment, although it may qualify in the same way as other investment for more general financial support through the grants given for new equipment in Development Areas.

10. Discharges of waste substances to the environment will always be with us; indeed, given the ability of the environment to receive and assimilate or dissipate these wastes, this can be an entirely legitimate and sensible use of resources. Through sensible physical planning and forethought about the environmental

---

*Product standards set levels of pollutants or nuisances not to be exceeded in the composition or in the emissions of a product, eg motor vehicle noise; specify properties or characteristics of design of a product, eg vehicle design; or are concerned with the way in which products are used. Emission standards are set for stationary installations and set levels of pollutants or nuisances not to be exceeded in liquid or gaseous emissions from such installations.

3

impact of different kinds of development it is possible greatly to reduce the nuisance value of such discharges.

11. The effectiveness of preventive planning, of liaison between authorities and of subsequent control measures must depend very largely on the quality of the information about local problems, about pollution trends and the way they are monitored and assessed and about possible solutions which authorities have available to them. Thus an effective monitoring and assessment system is fundamental to any pollution control policy. Information is needed on existing pollutant concentrations, long-term trends and the significance of new emissions in order to assess where hazards lie and where to concentrate resources. In Britain monitoring and assessment, like legislation, have developed piecemeal as the need arose. As a result considerable monitoring and assessment take place, but programmes are not always well co-ordinated and may not provide information in a form that is readily usable at both local and national level.

12. The Government issued a report in 1974 on "The Monitoring of the Environment in the United Kingdom" and has set up a series of sectoral monitoring management groups, for air, freshwater, marine water and land, to ensure that all the monitoring programmes are designed to produce useful information on existing pollution levels and long-term trends in a form that can readily be used at all policy levels. In addition two cross-sectoral management groups have been formed to build a medical and biological dimension into the monitoring and assessment system so that the health and ecological risks associated with particular levels, concentrations or combinations of existing or new pollutants can be assessed. The formation of these groups is a first step towards the development of a comprehensive, flexible and unified monitoring system. Their work is co-ordinated by a Steering Committee. Individual groups are considered in more detail in later chapters.

13. Research also has a vital role to play in the control of pollution, both by determining potential hazardous pollutants and by establishing methods of control, and the Government sponsors a considerable amount of work in this field, both in its own research establishments and in hospitals, universities, etc.

14. Pollution control has achieved many successes in the past—smoke control has led to a considerable improvement in the quality of air in our cities, and many rivers, such as the Thames, have been cleaned up—but new problems continually arise. Current preoccupations range for example from emissions from vehicles on motorways to pollution from heavy metals generally, and to deal with these and future problems the control system must continually evolve.

15. In 1970 the standing Royal Commission on Environmental Pollution was established "to advise on matters, both national and international, concerning the pollution of the environment; on the adequacy of research in this field; and the future possibilities of danger to the environment". The Royal Commission has published reports on several different aspects of environmental pollution.

16. Pollution mainly affects the country in which it arises, but it may pass to

other countries through a variety of media. For example, pollutants in air can be carried by the winds, or marine pollution may affect the shared seas. Also, traded articles may be subject to different pollution controls by manufacturing and importing countries. For these reasons a variety of international controls have been developed. These are considered further in the following chapters, particularly in Chapter 9.

CHAPTER 2

AIR POLLUTION

I. INTRODUCTION

17. The development of air pollution control in Great Britain has been essentially pragmatic. As an early industrial country Britians has generally built up her law and administration stage by stage in response to particular problems. As a result the law relating to air pollution is to be found in a number of statutes, while the administrative arrangements are a blend of central direction and local discretion, based on the principle of "best practicable means" mentioned in Chapter 1.

II. ADMINISTRATIVE ARRANGEMENTS

18. Certain processes that give rise to particularly noxious or offensive emissions, or are technically difficult to control, are regulated in England and Wales by the Health and Safety Executive (HSE) through HM Alkali and Clean Air Inspectorate. In Scotland similar functions are exercised by HM Industrial Pollution Inspectorate (HMIPI) on behalf of the Health and Safety Commission, under an agency agreement with the Secretary of State for Scotland. Controls cover over 60 processes in the chemical, metal manufacturing, ceramic and allied industries, production and processing of ammonia, cement and brick works, and the generation of electricity by combustion of fossil fuel.

19. Most other forms of air pollution come under the control of local authorities, advised by central Government and the Alkali Inspectorate (or, in Scotland, HMIPI). The local authorities control domestic emissions and emissions from commercial and industrial processes not within the scope of the Alkali Inspectorate. The Department of Transport (DTp) is responsible for legislation to control pollution by motor vehicles. Emissions from aircraft are controlled by the Department of Trade (DT).

III. LEGISLATION

20. The principal statutes governing air pollution are as follows:

   (a) Alkali etc Works Regulation Act 1906
   (b) Health and Safety at Work etc Act 1974
   (c) Public Health Acts 1936 and 1961, Public Health (Recurring Nuisances) Act 1969 and Public Health (Scotland) Act 1897
   (d) Clean Air Acts 1956 and 1968
   (e) Radioactive Substances Act 1960

6

(f) Control of Pollution Act 1974

(g) Road Traffic Acts 1972 and 1974.

Most of the legislation applies equally to the whole of Great Britain, but there are minor variations for Scotland.

Alkali etc Works Regulation Act 1906

21. The emissions from certain chemical and industrial processes have long been subject to special control because they were considered to be particularly dangerous or offensive or technically difficult to regulate. The first process to be singled out in this way was the production of alkali, which gave rise to huge emissions of hydrochloric acid gas. The Alkali Act of 1863 took its name from this process. The Act was extended subsequently to cover other processes, until the legislation was consolidated in the Alkali etc Works Regulation Act 1906 which remained the governing statute until 1974, when it was partly subsumed by the Health and Safety at Work etc Act 1974. Further processes have been added by Order and there are now over 60 processes, involving some 2,200 works and 3,700 operations registrable under the Act. Certain sections of the Act were repealed when the relevant parts of the Control of Pollution Act 1974 and the Health and Safety at Work etc Act 1974 were brought into effect.

22. Responsibility for enforcing the Alkali Act belongs in England and Wales to the Alkali and Clean Air Inspectorate, and in Scotland to HMIPI. The Alkali Act specifies emission limits for only four processes. So far as other processes are concerned the Inspectorates work to the concept that best practicable means should be used to ensure that potentially dangerous or offensive emissions are not discharged except in a harmless or inoffensive form. For some processes emission limits and operating procedures are laid down by the Inspectorates after discussions with industry, and adherence to these limits is accepted by the Inspectorates as evidence that best practicable means are being observed. These limits are altered from time to time as new techniques for control are developed or because of changing circumstances. The obligation to comply with best practicable means is a continuing one and regular inspections and tests are carried out by the Inspectorates to ensure that they are met.

Health and Safety at Work etc Act 1974

23. The Health and Safety at Work etc Act 1974 set up the Health and Safety Commission and charged it with ensuring the health, safety and welfare of persons at work and with protecting others against risks to health and safety in connection with the activities of persons at work. Its responsibility in the field of control of emissions to the atmosphere is limited by section 1(1)(d) to such classes of premises as are prescribed by regulations made under the Act. Section 5(1) of the Act places on any person having control of any premises

of a class prescribed under section 1(1)(d) the general duty to use the best practicable means for preventing the emission into the atmosphere of noxious or offensive substances and for rendering harmless or inoffensive such substances as may be so emitted. "Means" includes the manner in which any plant provided for the purpose is used and the supervision of any operation giving rise to noxious or offensive emissions. "Noxious or offensive" is not defined exclusively in the Act, although section 5(3) empowers the Secretary of State to declare in regulations that certain substances shall be deemed to be included within the term. No such regulations have been made to date.

24. The Health and Safety Commission is appointed by the Secretary of State for Employment, although the Secretaries of State for the Environment, for Wales and for Scotland ensure and are answerable to Parliament for the adequacy of measures taken by the Commission for the control of emissions into the atmosphere of noxious or offensive substances from prescribed classes of premises, and they exercise the Secretary of State's powers to make regulations on these matters. The day to day operations of the Commission are conducted by the Health and Safety Executive (HSE), which it appoints. The Executive in turn may appoint such inspectors as it requires. The Alkali and Clean Air Inspectorate was transferred on 1 January 1975 from DOE to the Executive; but it remains an identifiable unit and retains its title. There are some 40 Alkali Inspectors under a Chief Inspector. (Other inspectorates transferred to HSE under the Act were the Factory, Mines and Quarries, Explosives and Nuclear Installations Inspectorates.) In Scotland HMIPI has some 10 inspectors under a Chief Inspector.

25. The 1974 Act confers on all inspectors appointed under it wide powers to enter and inspect premises, to require improvements to be made and in cases of imminent danger to order the cessation of the activity in question.

Public Health Acts

26. In contrast to the legislation described in the previous section which deals with specific processes, the Public Health Acts are much wider in their application. They are enforced by the local authorities and are the primary weapon against noxious or offensive emissions (other than smoke, grit and dust) from premises not dealt with under specific legislation. Part III of the Public Health Act 1936 (or Part II of the Public Health (Scotland) Act 1897) places on every district council or London borough the duty to inspect its district for nuisances and if they are found to take action to require their abatement. Nuisances include "any dust or effluvia caused by any trade, business, manufacture or process and being prejudicial to the health of or a nuisance to the inhabitants of the district". If a local authority is satisfied that a nuisance exists it must serve on the person responsible a notice requiring him to take whatever steps (including closure or carrying out remedial measures) are necessary to abate the nuisance. If he fails to comply with the notice the local authority may apply to the Magistrates' Court for a nuisance order commanding compliance,

and on conviction the court may also impose a fine not exceeding £200. A nuisance order may still be made under the Public Health (Recurring Nuisances) Act 1969 even though the nuisance has abated, if the court is satisfied that it is likely to recur. The local authority may itself do any work necessary to implement the order and recover the cost from the person responsible. Any person aggrieved by a nuisance may apply direct to the Magistrates' Court for an order without waiting for the local authority to act. Similar provisions apply to control of nuisances in Scotland by islands and district councils and ratepayers who are aggrieved by the nuisance may requisition the local authority which may, if it thinks fit, petition the Sheriff. There is no provision in Scottish legislation for direct application to the Sheriff except in the case of the local authority failing to carry out its duty in terms of the Act.

27. It is a defence to certain nuisance order proceedings in the Magistrates' Court, including those in respect of dust or effluvia, that the best practicable means were being used to prevent nuisance. The local authority (in England and Wales) may, however, elect to proceed in the High Court in which event the use of best practicable means is not a conclusive defence. In England an application may not be made by a local authrity in the Magistrates' Court for a nuisance order against a works controlled by the Alakli Inspectorate without the consent of the Secretary of State for the Environment (or in Wales, the Secretary of State for Wales). Scottish local authorities may elect to cause proceedings to be taken in the Court of Session as an alternative to the Sheriff Court but the taking of best practicable means is a conclusive defence in either Court (section 36 of the Public Health (Scotland) Act 1897).

28. Certain trades, mainly concerned with the processing of animal residues, are expressly declared in the Public Health Acts to be "offensive trades". Such trades may be carried on only with the consent of and in accordance with any byelaws made by the local authority. Such byelaws must be approved by the Secretary of State.

Clean Air Acts 1956 and 1968

29. These Acts replaced and extended the provisions relating to smoke nuisances in the Public Health Acts, and control certain emissions from industrial combustion processes not within the scope of the Alkali Inspectorate or HMIPI in Scotland. Dark smoke may not be emitted from any trade or industrial premises or from the chimney of any building or from any railway engine or from any vessel in inland or estuarial waters or in port. The Secretary of State may by order relax these provisions and orders have been made to accommodate essential lighting up, soot blowing etc and to exempt (subject to conditions) certain activities where dark smoke is unavoidable.

30. Any new furnace (other than a domestic boiler with a maximum heating capacity of less than 55,000 Btu/per hour) must be capable so far as practicable of being operated continuously without emitting smoke when burning fuel of

the type for which it was designed. The local authority must be notified of any proposal to install a new furnace.

31. Any new furnace to burn pulverised fuel, or any other solid matter at a rate of 100 pounds or more per hour, or any liquid or gaseous matter at a rate of 1·25 million or more Btu per hour must be equipped to the satisfaction of the local authority with plant to arrest the emission of grit and dust. The Secretary of State may on appeal vary the local authority's requirements. The Secretary of State may by order exempt any class of furnace from the obligation to fit arrestment plant, and limited exemptions have been granted. The local authority may on application exempt an individual furnace, and should the application be refused there is a right of appeal to the Secretary of State. The local authority may also require the emission of grit, dust and fume from any furnace rated as above to be measured in accordance with procedures prescribed by the Secretary of State. If a new chimney is to be built to serve a new or existing furnace rated as above or an existing furnace so rated is enlarged, the height of the chimney must be approved by the local authority, who must be satisfied that it will be high enough to prevent the emissions becoming prejudicial to health or a nuisance. Again there is a right of appeal to the Secretary of State against the local authority's determination. The Secretary of State may by order prescribe limits on the rates of emission of grit and dust from the chimney of any furnace other than a domestic boiler with a heating capacity of less than 55,000 Btu per hour. This has now been done for many types of furnaces and further regulations to deal with other types are under consideration.

32. Section 11 of the 1956 Act empowers local authorities to make smoke control orders, which are subject to confirmation by the Secretary of State, prohibiting the emission of smoke from buildings, including dwellings, in any part of their districts. Specific buildings or fireplaces (which term includes any furnace, grate or stove) may be exempted in the order. Before the order may be confirmed it must be advertised and the Secretary of State must, if objections are made and not withdrawn, arrange for a local inquiry or hearing to be held. The Secretary of State may in regulations specify particular fuels or classes of fireplaces as being smokeless. A householder who as a result of a smoke control order has to change his means of cooking or heating may claim from the local authority a grant of 70% of the reasonable cost of installing suitable domestic smokeless appliances. The local authority may pay more than 70% if it wishes. The Secretary of State may (and normally does) reimburse the local authority four-sevenths of its grant. Well over one-third of the premises in England and Wales, including over 90% of those in Greater London, are reckoned now to be covered by orders. There are substantial variations between areas.

33. None of the aforementioned provisions of the Clean Air Acts applies to works controlled by the Alkali and Clean Air Inspectorate or HMIPI, unless the Secretary of State orders otherwise in respect of any particular premises under section 11(3) of the 1968 Act.

Radioactive Substances Act 1960

34. This Act is covered in Chapter 6 on radioactive substances.

Control of Pollution Act 1974

35. Part IV of this Act was implemented in England and Wales in January 1976. It extends the powers of local authorities to carry out investigations into air pollution by enabling them to obtain information about the emissions to the atmosphere from any premises other than private dwellings. The local authority may make arrangements with the occupier of the premises for either the occupier or the authority to carry out measurements, but the local authority may also require the occupier by notice to supply certain information. The kinds of information which may be demanded are to be prescribed in regulations made by the Secretary of State. The occupier will be free to appeal to the Secretary of State against a notice on the grounds that disclosure of the information would prejudice a trade secret or be contrary to the public interest or that the information could not be provided except at undue expense. Any information obtained by the local authority will (with certain exceptions) have to be kept in a register open to the public. Section 76 of the Act gives the Secretary of State new powers to limit or reduce air pollution by making regulations to control the sulphur content of oil fuel for furnaces or engines.

Emissions from Motor Vehicles

36. Emissions from motor vehicles are affected both by the structure of the vehicle and the composition of the fuel used (see paragraphs 23 and 27). Emissions from vehicles are controlled principally by the Motor Vehicles (Construction and Use) Regulations 1973 made under the 1972 Road Traffic Act. These regulations have for many years required motor vehicles to be so constructed that no avoidable smoke or visible vapour therefrom causes, or is likely to cause, injury to other road users or damage to property. There are other regulations dealing with specific parts of the vehicle or types of vehicle which are designed to reduce one or more of the different kinds of emission from vehicles (smoke, hydrocarbons, carbon monoxide).

37. Under section 53 of the Road Traffic Act 1972 authorised examiners are empowered to carry out checks at the roadside. Under section 45 of the Act all heavy goods vehicles (over 30 cwt unladen weight) must undergo an annual test by the Heavy Goods Vehicle Testing Stations. In both cases vehicle examiners are empowered to prohibit the further use of any vehicle considered to be in an unsatisfactory condition. Many such prohibitions are issued each year for smoke offences and are brought to the notice of Area Licensing Authorities when operators' licences are to be renewed. Other vehicles more than three years old must also undergo an annual test for certain safety requirements, but these do not include the rules about exhaust emissions. Enforcement of the latter is limited to spot checks by the police.

38. Attention is now being given to reducing pollution from vehicle exhausts

by regulating the contents of the fuel used, in particular lead. In 1971 the Government was advised by the Chief Medical Officer of the Department of Health and Social Security (DHSS) that, although the levels of lead emissions from vehicles at that time did not offer any significant danger to the community as a whole, it was desirable that such levels should not rise and should, if possible, be reduced. Two reductions have been voluntarily achieved in the maximum permitted level of lead in petrol which now rests at 0·55 grams per litre. A recent review of the medical evidence relating to lead in petrol and its effect on man's health concluded that it would be prudent to restrict total emissions of lead from cars to the 1971 levels. The Government accepted that advice. The maximum permitted lead content of petrol will be reduced to 0·50 grams per litre as soon as possible and to 0·45 grams per litre in 1978. Furthermore, the Government intends to set the standard at 0·40 grams per litre in 1981 to keep in harmony with general European standards. Section 75 of the Control of Pollution Act 1974 empowers the Secretary of State to make regulations to control the composition of motor fuels in order to limit or reduce air pollution; regulations made under this section will supersede voluntary agreements.

IV. ADVISORY BODIES

Clean Air Council

39. Under Section 23 of the Clean Air Act 1956 the Secretary of State for the Environment is required to appoint a consultative Clean Air Council to keep under review the progress made in abating air pollution in England and Wales and to render him advice. The Council numbers about 30 members, 2 of whom are appointed from Wales in consultation with the Secretary of State for Wales. In addition to monitoring the progress of domestic smoke control it has mounted investigations into particular aspects of air pollution from industry. The Council has also recently established four standing committees to expand its range of interests in clean air matters. Council recommendations concerning the publication of information about industrial emissions to the atmosphere formed the basis of provisions contained in Part IV of the Control of Pollution Act. The Secretary of State for Scotland appoints a Clean Air Council for Scotland with similar functions.

V. CENTRAL GOVERNMENT ADVICE

40. Advice is given by means of circulars and occasional more substantial publications—generally explanatory memoranda enclosed with the circulars. The main circulars are as follows:

MHLG 64/56 Clean Air Act 1956. Guidance on certain provisions of the Act
DHS 61/57 Clean Air Act 1956. Memorandum on miscellaneous provisions
of the Act

MHLG	24/58	Clean Air Act 1956. Dark smoke (permitted periods) regulations
	33/58	Clean Air Act 1956. Guidance on provisions
DHS	97/58	Clean Air Act 1956. Dark smoke regulations
DHS	28/59	Clean Air Act 1956. Memorandum on industrial provisions
MHLG	1/61	Clean Air Act 1956. Notification of provisional plans for establishing smoke control areas
	12/61	Air pollution. Measurement and research
SDD	11/63	Radioactive Substances Act 1960. Guidance on provisions
MHLG	69/63	Clean Air Act 1956. Smoke control areas
	51/65	Clean Air Act 1956. Grant arrangements (WO 14/65)
	69/65	Clean Air. Tall buildings and industrial emissions (WO 69/65)
	55/65	Alkali etc Works Regulation Act 1906 and Order 1966 (WO 40/66)
	50/67	Clean Air Act 1956. Memorandum on chimney heights (WO 44/67, SDD 73/67)
	52/67	Clean Air Act 1956. Grit and dust: standard levels of emissions from boiler and furnace chimneys and methods of measurement (WO 23/67, SDD 48/67)
	69/68	Clean Air Act 1968. Guidance on provisions (WO 62/68, SDD 8/69)
	2/69	Clean Air Act 1956. Memorandum on emissions from cold blast cupolas at iron foundries (WO 2/69, SDD 9/69)
	28/69	Clean Air Act 1968. Height of Chimneys Regulations (WO 23/69, SDD 25/69)
	54/69	Clean Air Act 1968. Guidance on provisions (WO 51/69, SDD 49/69)
	72/69	Clean Air Act 1968. Exemption regulations (WO 71/69, SDD 69/69)
SDD	67/70	Clean Air Acts 1956 and 1968. Guidance to provisions on chimney heights
DOE	2/71	Clean Air Acts 1956 and 1968. Regulations on Emissions of Grit and Dust from Furnaces (WO 2/71, SDD 25/71)
	35/71	Alkali etc Works Regulation Act 1906 and Order 1971 (WO 70/71)
SDD	105/72	Alkali etc Works Regulations (Scotland) Acts 1906 and 1951
DOE	6/73	Lead in the environment (WO 6/73)
SDD	40/73	Clean Air Acts 1956 and 1968. Domestic smoke control
DOE	115/74	Report on Lead in the Environment (WO 24/74)
	131/74	Clean Air Act 1956. Local Government Act 1972. Progress of smoke control (WO 206/74)
SDD	3/75	Health and Safety at Work etc Act 1974, Control of Pollution Act 1974
DOE	7/75	Control of Pollution Act 1974. Commencement Order No. 2. Amends the Alkali etc Works Regulation Act 1906 (WO 9/75)
	11/75	Health and Safety at Work etc Act 1974. Clean Air Enactments (Repeals and Modifications) Regulations 1974 (WO 16/75)

SDD	20/75	Clean Air Acts 1956 and 1968. Appliance cost limits
DOE	31/75	Clean Air Acts 1956 and 1968. Maximum cost limits (WO 50/75)
SDD	66/75	Clean Air Acts 1956 and 1968. Revised memorandum on smoke control areas
DOE	108/75	Clean Air. Interdepartmental Committee on Air Pollution Research. Information Services (WO 118/75)
	7/76	Control of Pollution Act 1974. Commencement Order No. 4 Part IV—Pollution of the atmosphere (WO 9/76)
	43/76	Control of smells from the animal waste processing industry (MAFF 76/CSAWP/1, WO 17/76)
	54/76	Clean Air Act. Smoke control areas. Revised grant arrangements.

41. The Alkali Inspectorate and HMIPI in Scotland keep in touch with local authorities in the course of their day to day work and from time to time the Inspectorates are asked for informal advice on the treatment of particular premises for which the local authorities are responsible. The advice of the Inspectorates is also freely available to all local planning authorities, not only on particular application for planning permission for new industrial premises or development in the vicinity of existing registered works, but also on matters of general planning, in order that they may take problems of atmospheric pollution fully into account when considering such proposals. The Factory Inspectorate also liaises with local authorities on pollution problems caused by contaminants arising as a result of factory processes and work activity generally.

VI. INTERNATIONAL ACTION

42. Within the European Economic Community (EEC) work is being carried out on various aspects of air pollution. Experts are discussing air quality criteria, and proposals to lay down air quality standards in respect of lead, sulphur dioxide and particulates have been made. Measures to control particular sources of pollution are also in hand. Already agreement has been reached on a directive concerning the sulphur content of gas oils, and proposals for a reduction of the lead content of petrol and for the sulphur content of fuel oil are under discussion.

43. The Organisation for Economic Co-operation and Development (OECD) and the Economic Commission for Europe (ECE) are also concerned with air pollution and are involved in studies of the long range transport of air pollutants.

VII. MONITORING

44. Both central and local Government are active in monitoring the state of the air. This is additional to the routine monitoring of emissions at source, which is carried out by industry, the Alkali Inspectorate and local authorities in the normal course of inspecting premises under their control. The biggest

single monitoring programme, and the only truly nationwide one, is the National Survey of Smoke and Sulphur Dioxide, comprising some 1,200 sites, mostly operated by local authorities. The information is collated by the Department of Industry's (DI) Warren Spring Laboratory (WSL) at Stevenage and published at intervals. Smaller scale programmes are measuring grit and dust, acid particles, aerosols, metals and vehicle emissions. Some local authorities also undertake ad hoc studies around particular works such as smelters. The Air Pollution Monitoring Management Group (referred to in paragraph 12) on which the central and local Government bodies concerned are represented, is currently considering how all this monitoring can be better co-ordinated in harmony with the work of the other five monitoring management groups. The United Kingdom also co-operates actively in international programmes for monitoring pollution which may have transfrontier implications and for sharing the results of research and experience generally.

VIII. RESEARCH

45. DOE promotes a great deal of research into specific topics of general application throughout the United Kingdom. Both the Welsh and Scottish Offices sponsor research into localised problems. WSL is the main centre in the general air pollution field, while the DOE Transport and Road Research Laboratory (TRRL) at Crowthorne is concerned with pollution from motor vehicles. The Ministry of Defence supports a wide range of research on topics related to air pollution, including aircraft engine exhausts, aspects of meteorology, and defence against chemical attack. Other work is done for DOE and DI at the Atomic Energy Research Establishment (AERE) Harwell and at various universities, and the Science Research Council (SRC) supports a range of more fundamental projects. The Medical Research Council (MRC), the Agricultural Research Council (ARC) and the Natural Environment Research Council (NERC) also support and carry out research into different aspects of the effects of air pollution, and MRC's Environmental Hazards Unit co-ordinates work on the health aspects of air pollution. In 1976 the Panel on Pollution Research of the Social Sciences Research Council (SSRC) completed a study of the role of the social scientist and priorities for social science research in the field of pollution.

46. The emphasis of Government sponsored research has tended to be on the impacts of air pollution and on its extent and behaviour after emission, but the Government has also sponsored research on the reduction and interception of emissions mainly in cases of general application, for example the effect of tall chimneys or high buildings on dispersion. TRRL carries out work on problems of vehicle design, and a major investigation into improved methods of odour prevention is being carried out at WSL. The bulk of research on abatement and control is, however, carried out by individual firms or trade associations. This is appropriate in that it accords with the polluter pays principle, and sensible in that the firm or industry concerned knows more about its production processes than any Government body can.

CHAPTER 3

FRESH-WATER POLLUTION

I. INTRODUCTION

47. The volume of water used in Great Britain has been rising at the rate of just over 2% a year. This is due to the increase in population, the clearance of slums resulting in modernisation of kitchens and bathrooms, the greater use of washing and dishwashing machines, the expansion of industry, and other small but cumulatively significant uses, such as car-washing and gardening. If this rate of increase persists, we shall be using at least 60% more water by the end of the century than we were using in 1974.

48. As more water is used domestically, industrially and agriculturally, more liquid waste will be discharged into sewers and rivers, and so rivers will contain an increasing proportion of sewage effluent and industrial waste. Although the amount of rain falling in this country is considerable (many times the total volume of water abstracted), much is lost through evaporation, transpiration by plants and run-off to the sea, and often the greater water demand is in the areas of lower rainfall. The variation in the incidence of water between wet and dry years can be as much as half of the average. In England and Wales public water supply is drawn from natural lakes and reservoirs, underground sources, and rivers, in roughly equal proportions. Thus about a third of water abstracted comes directly from rivers; these often contain a significant proportion of sewage effluent and industrial waste. Clearly the management of water through the treatment of sewage and the control of all discharges to the sewers and rivers is a matter of great importance if we are to maintain safe health standards in water abstracted for drinking. In Scotland public water supply comes almost entirely from unpolluted upland sources, but similar considerations apply for other reasons, such as the needs of industry for clean river water.

Sewage Treatment

49. More than 90% of the population of Great Britain is provided with main drainage and water authority sewage treatment works serve over four-fifths of the population. Although this proportion is higher than in any other country in the world, the position is not as satisfactory as it might seem, as many sewage works do not produce an effluent of an acceptable standard because they are old, in bad repair or simply heavily overloaded, although many new works have been completed in the last decade or so. In order just to maintain standards, let alone improve them, a substantial and continuing programme of capital investment would be required.

50. The object of modern methods of sewage treatment is to convert unstable sewage into an effluent which may be discharged to an adjacent watercourse

without significantly worsening conditions in that watercourse. The degree of treatment required prior to discharge and the standard of the effluent depend on local circumstances such as the quantity and quality of the receiving waters and the other uses to which these are put. In general the standards recommended by the Royal Commission on Sewage Disposal (1898–1915) are the normal minimum requirements for sewage effluent discharged to inland waters.

Industrial Discharges

51. The nature and strength of sewage is influenced by the type and proportion of the industrial effluents (including waste from farms) present in it along with the domestic sewage. On average the proportion of industrial effluent in sewage is about one-fifth, though in some areas it may be considerably higher than this. Certain trade wastes present great problems in the treatment of sewage, as some are toxic and can affect the biological processes employed during treatment at sewage works. To help in assessing the toxicity of effluents containing metals and other substances, the Water Research Centre (WRC) has established an information service (an index) on the effects of substances in terms of fish toxicity, biodegradability and other factors important in effluents. The index is continually revised and is available both to industry and to those responsible for water pollution control.

52. Although the pollution caused by farm waste is minor in comparison with that from industrial waste and sewage, it can aggravate problems by increasing pollution levels if it enters a watercourse. The problem has become more serious in recent years because the adoption of more intensive systems of livestock production has resulted in increased concentrations of housed animals on individual farms. This has led to increased volumes of manures on individual farms which require safe disposal. Most animal manures and waste produced on the farm are disposed of by spreading on the land, for if this is carried out efficiently these wastes are a valuable fertiliser. However, application of farm waste to the land can cause problems on surface run-off, leaching and seepage which can be serious under certain circumstances.

Accidental Discharges

53. Sewerage and industrial discharges are not, however, the only ways in which pollution can enter the water systems. There are also the dangers of run-offs from waste tips, leakages from storage tanks and accidents during the transport of hazardous chemicals. Where accidents occur involving toxic chemicals in transit emergency services can be helped to deal with potential hazards through the HAZCHEM Scheme, whereby tankers carry coded signs that identify the substance being transported and indicate what action should be taken in an emergency. Emergency services may obtain advice and assistance for dealing with the problem via the Chemical Industries Association "Chem-safe" scheme (see paragraph 114).

17

II. ADMINISTRATIVE ARRANGEMENTS

54. The Secretary of State for the Environment has a duty to promote a national policy for water and, in the context of water pollution control, to secure the effective execution of so much of the policy as relates to sewage and the treatment and disposal of sewage and other effluents, the restoration and maintenance of the wholesomeness of rivers and the enhancement and preservation of amenity in connection with inland water. The respective Secretaries of State exercise similar functions in Wales and Scotland. Policy matters relating to fisheries in inland and coastal waters are the province of the Minister of Agriculture, Fisheries and Food in England and Wales, and the Secretary of State for Scotland in Scotland.

Water Authorities

55. The water authorities established under the Water Act 1973 are autonomous bodies. Their responsibilities cover the management of all water services in England and Wales and include water conservation, water supplies, sewerage and sewage disposal, control of river pollution, maintenance, improvement and development of fisheries, land drainage and flood prevention and water recreation. Some of their powers and duties are broadly outlined below in the section on legislation.

56. A majority of the members of a water authority are appointed by the county and the district councils within its area in proportion to population. The other members are people with relevant or special knowledge who are appointed by the Secretary of State for the Environment or for Wales and the Minister of Agriculture, Fisheries and Food. Each water authority has a permanent staff of specialist officers and their assistants and is usually headed by a Chief Executive.

57. Although water authorities are financially self-supporting, deriving their revenue mainly from charges for services such as sewage disposal and water supply, overall financial control of public expenditure is exercised by the Government and each water authority is limited in the amount of capital expenditure it can incur. Each water authority submits annually to the Secretary of State and the Minister of Agriculture, Fisheries and Food a five-year rolling programme of proposed capital works, together with a published report giving details of the work done during the year and an outline of its future policy and programme.

Authorities in Scotland

58. In Scotland water supply and pollution control are the responsibilities of separate authorities. Water supply is the function of the nine regional councils and three islands councils established under the Local Government (Scotland) Act 1973, who are also responsible for sewerage and sewage disposal, and the Central Scotland Water Development Board.

59. The promotion of cleanliness of the waters in their areas was made the responsibility of river purification authorities under the Rivers (Prevention of Pollution) (Scotland) Act 1951. The authorities consisted of nine river purification boards, established under the Act, whose membership comprised representatives of the constituent local authorities and persons appointed by the Secretary of State for Scotland, and, in less populated areas in the north and west of Scotland, 12 local authorities. Under the Local Government (Scotland) Act 1973, seven river purification boards were established from 16 May 1975 covering the whole mainland, while the three islands councils became the responsible authorities in their areas.

III. LEGISLATION

60. The principal statutes governing fresh-water pollution are as follows:
- (a) Public Health Act 1936
- (b) Water Acts 1945 and 1948 and Water (Scotland) Act 1946
- (c) Public Health (Drainage of Trade Premises) Act 1937 and Public Health Act 1961 (Part V)
- (d) Salmon and Freshwater Fisheries (Protection) (Scotland) Act 1951 and Salmon and Freshwater Fisheries Act 1975
- (e) Rivers (Prevention of Pollution) Acts 1951 and 1961
- (f) Clean Rivers (Estuaries and Tidal Waters) Act 1960
- (g) Rivers (Prevention of Pollution) (Scotland) Acts 1951 and 1965
- (h) Water Resources Act 1963
- (i) Sewerage (Scotland) Act 1968
- (j) Water Act 1973
- (k) Water (Scotland) Act 1967 and Local Government (Scotland) Act 1973
- (l) Control of Pollution Act 1974.

Public Health Act, 1936

61. Section 15 of the Public Health Act 1936 empowers a water authority to construct public sewers and sewage treatment works and section 31 requires that the authority must exercise these functions without creating a nuisance. Under the Act it is an offence to discharge into a public sewer any matter (including steam or liquid at a temperature higher than 100°F and petroleum spirit (section 27)) likely to damage the sewer or the treatment process, or to throw or deposit ashes, bricks, rubbish, filth or any other matter likely to cause annoyance into any river or stream (section 259). Local authorities have powers under the Act to deal with ponds, pools, ditches, gutters and watercourses if these are in such a state as to be prejudicial to health or a nuisance.

Water Acts 1945 and 1948 and Water (Scotland) Act 1946

62. Under sections 18 and 19 of the 1945 Act water authorities can make bye-laws for preventing pollution of their water whether on the surface or under-

ground. Section 22 confers powers on water undertakers to acquire land and execute works for the protection of water which belongs to them. It is an offence under section 22 if by any act or neglect a source of water used for human consumption is polluted or likely to be polluted. There are similar provisions in the Water (Scotland) Act 1946.

Public Health (Drainage of Trade Premises) Act 1937 and Public Health Act 1961

63. These Acts are concerned with regulating discharges of trade effluents to the public sewers. The 1937 Act gives industrial dischargers a right, subject to the consent of the water authority, to drain into public sewers. In order to safeguard the fabric of the sewers, the treatment processes at sewage works and of course the condition of the waters to which the treated mixed effluents will ultimately be discharged, authorities are empowered to impose quality and quantity conditions on the discharges and to make charges for conveyance and treatment. There is provision for appeal to the Secretary of State against a refusal to give a consent or against any conditions imposed in a consent, including the charge levied for the conveyance and treatment of the trade effluent.

Salmon and Freshwater Fisheries Act 1975

64. Sections 4 and 5 of this Act prohibit any person from putting or knowingly permitting to be put into water containing fish any liquid or solid matter which will cause the water to be poisonous or injurious to fish or their spawning grounds. The Act also gives water authorities the power to make byelaws to regulate the deposit or discharge in any waters containing fish of any liquid or solid matter detrimental to salmon, trout or freshwater fish. It does not apply to Scotland.

Salmon and Freshwater Fisheries (Protection) (Scotland) Act 1951

65. The Act prohibits the use of poison or other noxious substances in or near any waters with the intent to take or destroy fish (although the use of such poison may be permitted by the Secretary of State for Scotland for scientific purposes) or for the purpose of protecting, improving or developing stocks of fish.

Rivers (Prevention of Pollution) Act 1951

66. Section 2 of this Act makes it an offence to cause or knowingly permit poisonous, noxious or polluting matter to enter a stream (defined to include any non-tidal watercourse or inland water, apart from sewers, or lakes or ponds not discharging to a stream). Section 7 prohibits new or altered outlets for discharges of industrial (including farm) or sewage effluents into streams and new discharges without the consent of the appropriate water authority. The authority can refuse consent or lay down conditions as to the quality and quantity to which a discharge has to comply. There is a right of appeal to the Secretary of State against the authority's decision. (This is now contained in

the 1961 Act (see paragraph 70).) The Secretary of State can, by order under section 6 of the Act, extend the provisions of the Act to specified tidal waters, estuaries and adjoining parts of the sea. A few minor estuaries are fully controlled by order. The condition of the tidal Thames has much improved in recent years and, through special legislation, has been under full control since 1968.

67. Many industrial dischargers and farmers have to treat their effluents, before discharging them into streams or rivers, to bring them up to the standard set by the water authority. Samples of any discharge may be taken by the water authority and penalties are provided in the Act for any contravention of the conditions in the consent to discharge or for polluting a stream or river. Where a water authority thinks that a contravention of section 2 is likely to occur it may apply to the court under section 3 of the Act for an order prohibiting the activity in question or permitting it only on terms designed to remove the grounds of complaint, or such other order as the court thinks fit. Consent to discharge from the sewage disposal works of water authorities is given by the Secretary of State.

68. The water authorities are also empowered to make byelaws under section 5 of the Act, subject to confirmation by the Secretary of State and the Minister of Agriculture, Fisheries and Food, to prevent rubbish, litter etc being put into streams or rivers and to control the use of vessels fitted with sanitary appliances from which polluting matter can pass into the stream.

Clean Rivers (Estuaries and Tidal Waters) Act 1960

69. The 1951 Act originally applied only to non-tidal waters, but this Act also brought under control new or altered discharges to most estuaries.

Rivers (Prevention of Pollution Act) 1961

70. This Act strengthened the 1951 Act by bringing under control the pre-1951 discharges for which specific consent had not been required under that Act. Each discharge, whether commenced before 1951 or after, is now treated on its individual merits taking into account the effect on the river to which it is to be made. Conditions imposed by a water authority must be reviewed periodically under section 5 of the 1961 Act. The discharger of effluents has the right of appeal to the Secretary of State against any refusal by a water authority to allow a discharge or against any condition imposed by the authority. Discharges commenced before 1951 became unlawful on 1 June 1963 if no application for a consent to discharge had by then been made to the water authority. The Act did not bring under control existing discharges to tidal waters and estuaries but the provisions of section 6 of the 1951 Act, whereby specific tidal waters or parts of the sea could be controlled by order made by the Secretary of State, were extended by section 9 of the 1961 Act so that existing discharges as well as new ones could be controlled in a specified area.

Rivers (Prevention of Pollution) (Scotland) Acts 1951 and 1965

71. The 1951 Act gave the Secretary of State for Scotland (advised by the Scottish River Purification Advisory Committee) the duty to promote the cleanliness of the rivers and other inland and tidal waters of Scotland. It also gave river purification authorities a duty to exercise the functions conferred on them by the same Act to promote the cleanliness of the waters in their areas and to conserve so far as possible the water resources of their areas.

72. The functions conferred on the river purification authorities relate to the regulation of new or altered discharges after the river purification authority for any area was constituted. The 1965 Act extended this control from 2 November 1966 to cover all discharges to inland waters and new discharges to certain areas of tidal waters and controlled waters specified in a schedule to the Act.

73. The Secretary of State has made tidal waters orders under the 1951 Act which enable river purification authorities to control new discharges to tidal waters in certain areas (and existing discharges after the 1965 Act). These orders cover the main estuaries of the Clyde, Forth and Tay, waters off the coastlines of Solway, Ayrshire, Banff, Moray and Nairn, and minor areas sensitive to pollution like Findhorn Bay and Wick Bay. Scotland's water pollution problems are concentrated, like the population, in the central belt; accordingly a considerable programme of improvements to sewerage and sewage treatment works has centred on the Forth and Clyde estuaries, and the areas draining to them.

Water Resources Act 1963

74. This Act established a Water Resources Board and *river authorities in England and Wales. Provision was also made under sections 72 and 73 for the prevention of pollution of underground water by discharges into any well, pipe or borehole. Emergency powers to clear accidental pollution of rivers were granted under section 76; section 68 empowered river authorities to acquire land, either by agreement or compulsorily, for the purpose of protecting against pollution water in any reservoir owned or operated by them or in any underground strata from which they were licensed to take water.

Sewerage (Scotland) Act 1968

75. The Sewerage (Scotland) Act 1968 places a duty on regional and islands councils to provide such public sewers as may be necessary for effectually draining their areas of domestic sewage, surface water and trade effluent. The councils also have a duty to make provision, by means of sewage treatment works or otherwise, for dealing with the contents of the sewers.

---

*These replaced the river boards set up in 1948 and were in turn replaced by the water authorities in 1974.

Water Act 1973

76. Based largely on the recommendations of the Central Advisory Water Committee, this Act was responsible for the re-organisation of the water industry in England and Wales. On 1 April 1974, nine regional water authorities in England and the Welsh National Water Development Authority became responsible for the functions of water supply, sewerage, sewage treatment, the management and development and control of rivers and aquifers and all uses of water associated with them, land drainage and flood prevention and fisheries. Previously these duties had been shared between some 200 water undertakings, 1,400 local authorities and 29 river authorities. For the first time England and Wales had single authorities each responsible within its own area for all aspects of the water cycle. The re-organisation left water companies in being but as agents of the water authorities and similarly sewerage (but not sewage treatment and disposal) is managed under agreement by most district councils and London boroughs for the water authorities. The water authorities were also given important new functions in relation to recreation and amenity. In this they are advised by the Water Space Amenity Commission.

Water (Scotland) Act 1967 and Local Government (Scotland) Act 1973

77. In Scotland re-organisation took place on 16 May 1975, when the 13 Water Boards established under the Water (Scotland) Act 1967 were abolished and responsibilities for water supply, sewerage and sewage disposal were taken over by the new local authorities comprising nine regional and three islands councils.

Control of Pollution Act 1974

78. Part II of the Control of Pollution Act 1974 contains a number of provisions that will considerably strengthen existing legislation on the control of water pollution. The Act applies to Scotland as well as to England and Wales. When implemented, this part of the Act will extend current legislative controls to include nearly all discharges to inland and coastal waters (including underground waters that may be specified in regulations) and also to land, since substances discharged to land frequently find their way into water. Controls which previously covered only non-tidal waters, unless a tidal waters order had been made, will be extended to cover discharges through pipelines to tidal waters or the sea and discharges from working mines (which were previously exempt). Virtually all forms of water pollution are covered by the Act, in addition to the controls over discharges already mentioned.

79. Broadly the Act ensures that all *discharges* (regular or continuous activity involving draining effluents through fixed outlets) of trade or sewage effluent made to rivers, the sea, specified underground waters, or land are subject to the control of the appropriate water authority (river purification authority in Scotland) which may refuse the discharge or accept it subject to any reasonable

conditions. Pollution may, however, be caused by some casual or spontaneous activity not covered by the understanding of the term *discharge* and for which control by consent is neither practical nor desirable—for example the dumping of containers of chemical waste into a river. The Act refers to these as *entries* of poisonous, noxious or polluting matter, and severe penalties are available for those convicted of causing such an entry. In England and Wales applications for consent to discharge effluent into water or on to land will be made, as under the present system, to the water authority.

80. The discharger will have to provide details of the place where the discharge is to be made, the nature, composition and temperature of the proposed discharge and the daily amount and maximum rate of discharge. These details must then be advertised and after three months the water authority must reach a decision taking into account any objections to the scheme which have been raised. Appeals against this decision will be decided by the Secretary of State. Consents to discharge effluents, and the conditions attached to the consent, will be reviewed by the water authority from time to time.

81. The water authorities, who are themselves responsible for the larger proportion of effluent discharges into watercourses (from sewers and sewage works), will also have to undergo a similar procedure, with applications made to the Secretary of State. Water authorities will be required to maintain registers containing among other things prescribed particulars of applications for consents to discharge effluents; of consents issued and conditions attaching to them; of samples and analyses of effluents and receiving waters; and of notices restricting certain agricultural practices to prevent the pollution of water. The registers will be open to the public.

82. Under the Act stricter measures can be introduced to control accidental pollution. There are powers for the Secretary of State to make regulations so that anyone in control of a polluting substance must take certain specified precautions to prevent it from getting into water.

83. The water authorities will have powers and duties to forestall and remedy pollution of water, returning the stream and its flora and fauna to their previous state, and, if the pollution has been caused by an illegal discharge, to send the bill to the polluter. If the polluting discharge was within the conditions set by the water authority and the consent is not due for review, then the water authority must bear the costs of the remedial work and, if it is necessary to change the conditions of consent, may be liable to compensate the discharger.

84. The legislation is, of course, primarily concerned with preventing or controlling pollution from the disposal of waste or surplus material, but the position with agriculture is rather different. Normal farming practices may sometimes result in water pollution and farmers are therefore afforded some protection by the Act. Briefly, so long as the farmer pursues "good agricultural practice"* in going about his business he is protected from prosecution under section 31 of the Act. However, there is provision for a new procedure whereby

24

this protection may be withdrawn if the water authority can convince the Secretary of State that pollution has been or may be caused by a particular activity, in which case a notice will be served on the farmer concerned. Where a notice is served, the "good agricultural practice" protection is removed after a period of 28 days and the farmer will be open to prosecution in the same way as anyone else if he continues with the particular practice and it causes pollution.

85. Section 33 provides that after 1978 boats with sanitary appliances designed to discharge sewage directly into the water will no longer be allowed on inland waterways unless the appliance is sealed. At present this control may be selectively applied through byelaws. (Alternative sanitary arrangements will be made available for boat users.) This step has been taken largely to improve the rivers from an aesthetic and amenity point of view as the discharge of raw sewage often created unpleasant conditions for river users.

86. Under the 1974 Act penalties will be substantially increased. For most offences a person convicted in a Magistrates' Court will be subject to imprisonment for up to three months or fines of up to £400 or both; conviction in a higher court (trial by jury) will lead to imprisonment for up to two years, or a fine (there is no limit in this case) or both. When Part II of the Act has been fully implemented it will replace earlier legislation which will then be repealed. The Rivers (Prevention of Pollution) Act 1951 and the Clean Rivers (Estuaries and Tidal Waters) Act 1960 will be wholly repealed; the Rivers (Prevention of Pollution) (Scotland) Acts 1951 and 1965 and the Rivers (Prevention of Pollution) Act 1961 will be largely repealed.

IV. CENTRAL AND ADVISORY BODIES

The National Water Council

87. The National Water Council, which has advisory as well as other functions, was set up by the Water Act 1973 and consists of a Chairman appointed by the Secretary of State, the chairmen of the ten water authorities and ten other members appointed by the Secretary of State and the Minister of Agriculture, Fisheries and Food. The functions of the Council are to:

(a) advise any Minister on any matter relating to the national policy for water, and consider and advise any Minister and the water authorities on any matter of common interest to them;

(b) promote and assist the efficient performance by water authorities of their functions, in particular relating to research and forward planning;

(c) consider and advise any Minister on any matter on which the Council is consulted;

---

*The Minister of Agriculture, Fisheries and Food and the Secretary of State for Scotland approve codes of recommended agricultural practice.

(d) consult with interested organisations with a view to the establishment of a scheme throughout the United Kingdom for the testing and approval of water fittings to prevent the waste, misuse or contamination of water;

(e) prepare a scheme for training and education in connection with the services provided by the water authorities in England and Wales and the corresponding services in Scotland and Northern Ireland.

88. The Government has undertaken a full review of the general structure of the water industry and the charging policies it should follow.

89. Various joint technical committees have been set up to advise DOE and the National Water Council on technical aspects of water policy, research requirements and the implementation of research results in particular fields. Those whose work is closely related to water pollution control include:

(a) the Standing Technical Advisory Committee on Water Quality (STACWQ), which advises on the quality of river, estuarial and coastal waters and of water supplied for human consumption, agriculture and industry;

(b) the Standing Committee on the Disposal of Sewage Sludge;

(c) the Standing Technical Committee on Synthetic Detergents, which advises on standards of biodegradability of detergent (there is a voluntary agreement with detergent manufacturers to use "soft" detergents with at least 90% biodegradability—ie the undegraded residue entering rivers etc after treatment of sewage is less than 10%);

(d) the Standing Committee of Analysts;

(e) the Standing Committee on Water Reclamation.

In addition a Joint Committee on Medical Aspects of Water Quality has been set up between DOE and DHSS.

V. CENTRAL GOVERNMENT ADVICE

90. The main Government circulars issued on fresh-water pollution are:

MHLG	20/61	Pollution of water by tipped refuse
	46/61	Public Health Act 1961
	52/62	Liaison between planning authorities and river boards
SDD	40/65	Rivers (Prevention of Pollution) (Scotland) Act 1965
	27/66	Rivers (Prevention of Pollution) (Scotland) Act 1965
MHLG	37/66	Sewage effluents (WO 44/66, SDD 22/67)
	53/66	Revised model byelaws for prevention of waste, undue consumption, misuse or contamination of water
	63/67	Trade and sewage effluents (WO 57/67, SDD 58/67)
	64/68	Industrial effluents (WO 54/68)
	94/69	Surface water run-off from developments (WO 97/69)
	8/70	Standard tests for effluents—fish toxicity test (WO 8/70)

MHLG 12/70   Storm overflows and the disposal of storm sewage, Final report of the Technical Committee (WO 15/70, SDD 12/70)

44/70   Clean rivers (WO 46/70)

DOE   92/71   Reorganisation of the water and sewage services (WO 234/71)

10/72   Report of the Working Party on Sewage Disposal (WO 18/72, SDD 12/72)

SDD   20/72   Sewerage (Scotland) Act 1968

DOE   94/72   Inland oil spills (WO 156/72, SDD 114/72)

112/72   Analysis of raw, potable and waste waters (WO 244/72)

100/73   Water Act 1973

120/73   Water services reorganisation (WO 228/73)

163/74   Report of a River Pollution Survey of England and Wales 1973. Vol. 3 (WO 229/74)

20/75   Annual Report of the Steering Committee on Water Quality (WO 31/75)

127/75   River Pollution Survey report. Updated 1973. River quality and discharges of sewage and industrial effluents (WO 201/75).

VI. INTERNATIONAL ACTION

91. The EEC is developing a series of directives concerned with improving the quality of water. These directives establish appropriate quality objectives in relation to the water's intended use. Directives on the quality of surface water intended for abstraction for drinking water and on the quality of fresh and sea water in bathing areas have already been adopted. A draft directive on the quality of drinking water is under consideration.

92. The EEC Commission is also concerned to take direct action to reduce pollution from particular sources. Proposals are under discussion at the moment for directives on water pollution from pulp mills and from the waste products of the titanium dioxide industry. Two directives concerned with the levels of biodegradability of detergents have been adopted. Another directive (adopted on 3 May 1976) provides a framework within the Community for the control of water pollution by particularly dangerous substances. Both uniform emission limits for the substances concerned, and limits for their concentration in the receiving environment, will be set and member states will be able to adopt whichever they consider the more suitable.

VII. MONITORING

The River Pollution Survey

93. A survey of the rivers in England and Wales, showing the degrees of water pollution suffered, was carried out in 1970 and plans were made to repeat this on a regular basis.* The 1970 River Pollution Survey covered 4,500 rivers

---

*From 1973 the Survey will be updated every two years.

(roughly 24,000 miles altogether). Volume 1 covered river quality and showed that 76% of the length of non-tidal rivers in England and Wales was free from pollution. This compared with 73% shown in a similar (unpublished) survey in 1958. Other comparisons showed lengths of rivers:

	1958 compared with 1970	
(a) grossly polluted	6·4%	4·3%
(b) of poor quality, requiring urgent improvement	6·4%	4·8%
(c) of doubtful quality and needing improvement	14·3%	14·7%

The worst polluted stretches are, as one would expect, below dense concentrations of population and industry and often in the lower reaches where river flows are heaviest. The information was updated in 1972 and again in 1973 and showed a continued improvement in river quality.

94. Volume 2 of the survey was published in October 1972. This detailed the causes of river pollution, classified all discharges of industrial and sewage effluent into rivers and canals, gave details of discharges of crude sewage and unsatisfactory storm overflows and forecast the possibilities of river improvement in the future. This volume also included the report of a supplementary survey by the Confederation of British Industry which gave the first comprehensive account of the methods of disposal and cost of treatment of industrial effluent, analysed by type of industry. Excluding cooling water, some 4,000 million gallons per day of sewage and industrial effluent and water from mines are discharged to rivers. The expenditure to bring all discharges up to the standard considered attainable by 1980 would be about £610 million (at 1970 prices). The information in volume 2 was also updated to January 1972 and January 1973 and showed that small but significant improvements had taken place since 1970 in the quality of effluents discharged to rivers. Volume 3 was published in November 1974, covering the nine estuaries which were not previously covered and completing the survey. This means that now all rivers and controlled tidal waters have been surveyed; this is probably one of the most comprehensive surveys completed by any country. Its purpose is to provide an authentic means by which progress in combating water pollution can be measured.

95. A river pollution survey of Scotland ("Towards Cleaner Water") published in 1972 showed that only about 8% of the length of Scottish rivers, including tidal stretches, were either grossly polluted or of poor quality. However, in the central belt—Lothians, Forth, Clyde and Ayrshire—about 20% of the major rivers were in these categories. A subsequent report "Towards Cleaner Water —1975" presents a much more detailed picture. Of all rivers in the central belt only 5% are in the two more polluted categories, while the percentage of major rivers so classified has declined significantly. The report gives biological data on river quality and details of major discharges made to rivers, estuaries and the sea.

96. Monitoring for fresh water pollutants is carried out at various stages:

   (a) on discharge to sewers or rivers, by the industry concerned and by the local authority or water authority;

   (b) in streams and rivers, by the water authorities;

   (c) in fish, to determine levels of metals and pesticides, by the water authorities, the Ministry of Agriculture, Fisheries and Food, the Natural Environment Research Council (NERC) and the UK Atomic Energy Authority; and

   (d) in water abstracted for supply to homes and industry, by the water supply undertakings.

97. The report on "the Monitoring of the Environment in the United Kingdom" recommended the improved co-ordination and harmonisation of water monitoring by the different water authorities and the establishment of a national monitoring network to measure a wide range of substances. DOE has established a Freshwater Pollution Monitoring Management Group, one of the sectoral Monitoring Management Groups referred to in paragraph 12, which also functions as a Freshwater Monitoring Sub-Committee of STACWQ. It reports both to the Central Unit on Environmental Pollution and to STACWQ and DOE.

98. The Water Data Unit (part of DOE) has the function of collecting, processing and presenting data related to water services in England and Wales.

VIII. RESEARCH

99. Responsibilities for research into water pollution in the United Kingdom are distributed between Government, the water industry and a number of other institutions. Interests in the field often overlap, but, very broadly, the water industry is considered responsible for water pollution research which specifically concerns its water supply and sewage disposal functions or which has purely local relevance; DOE and the Scottish Development Department support a complementary programme on topics relevant to their national policy responsibilities for water, which include the abatement of pollution. Both programmes are supplemented by work commissioned by specialist bodies such as the Central Water Planning Unit (part of DOE) which is concerned with water quality, ecological studies of estuaries and environmental aspects of rivers and river waters. The MAFF Salmon and Freshwater Fisheries Laboratory and the Department of Agriculture and Fisheries for Scotland Freshwater Fisheries Laboratory undertake research into the effects of pollutants on freshwater fish. In addition the Research Councils (and particularly NERC) support research into the fundamental processes and mechanism involved in the whole field of freshwater and marine pollution.

100. The water industry carries out most of its research jointly through the Water Research Centre (WRC). Set up when water services were reorganised on 1 April 1974, the WRC is an industrial research association whose membership

is drawn from the whole of the industry and includes the 10 water authorities: it was formed by the amalgamation of the former Water Research Association with the former Water Pollution Research Laboratory and the major part of the technology divisions of the now defunct Water Resources Board. The Centre undertakes contract work for members and other individual customers in addition to its co-operative programme. DOE supports parts of the Centre's co-operative programme in which it has policy interests by means of selective area grants and places a major part of its own research programme with the Centre as contract work.

101. Current work on water pollution control aims principally to safeguard waters which receive effluents by improving conventional methods of sewage and trade effluent treatment and investigating alternative ones, backing this effort with research on modelling and monitoring methods concerned with the quality of water sources. Investigations range in scope from laboratory studies to large-scale development work.

CHAPTER 4

MARINE POLLUTION

I. INTRODUCTION

102. Marine pollution is defined by the United Nations Group of Experts on Scientific Aspects of Marine Pollution as "The introduction by man, directly or indirectly, of substances or energy into the marine environment (including estuaries) resulting in such deleterious effects as harm to living resources, hazard to human health, hindrance to marine activities including fishing, impairment of quality for use of sea water and reduction of amenities". This definition distinguishes between pollution, which is harmful, and the harmless introduction of substances or energy by man. In the view of the United Kingdom it is reasonable to utilise the natural capacity of the marine environment to accept and degrade many potential pollutants, and it is the aim of pollution control to permit such utilisation whilst preventing pollution. Pollutants may reach the sea by a variety of routes—through discharges from shipping, either operational (mainly oil) or accidental (oil and chemicals); as a result of sea-bed exploitation, either operational or accidental; through dumping of waste at sea; through discharges from land by means of rivers and pipelines; and from other sources, eg atmospheric deposition. Pollution reaching the sea via the rivers or the air is considered in other chapters on fresh water and air pollution, pesticides and radioactivity.

103. Pollution from ships includes both accidental and deliberate discharges of oil, sewage etc or chemicals from ships. Deliberate discharges occur, for example, when tankers clean out their tanks at sea; pollution can also result from accidents to tankers (eg the Torrey Canyon) but these are fortunately rare. The discharge by vessels of sewage or garbage usually has negligible effects except in confined seas or channels.

104. S nce pollution from ships often occurs beyond the limits of national jurisdiction, and since ships of many different states are involved, it is controlled largely by international conventions administered by the Inter-Governmental Maritime Consultative Organisation (IMCO), and implemented on a national level by domestic legislation. The first conventions were concerned solely with pollution by oil, but recent developments have extended the system to other harmful substances (see section VI).

105. Exploration and exploitation of sea-bed resources on the UK continental shelf are at present confined to dredging for sand and gravel and to off-shore operations for gas and oil. These are so far controlled by national rather than international regulations.

106. Dumping at sea is defined in the Dumping at Sea Act 1974 as the permanent

deposit of substances or articles below high-water mark from a vehicle, ship, aircraft, hovercraft or marine structure or from a structure on land designed for the purpose of depositing solids in the sea. It does not cover discharges through pipelines or discharges incidental to or derived from the normal operation of ships etc except where its normal operation is to dispose of waste. Most materials are disposed of some distance from the coast and outside territorial waters although quantities of sewage sludge and dredging spoil are dumped in coastal waters. Dumping at sea is subject to various international controls (see section VI). There will be no general controls over discharges to the sea or estuaries from land until the relevant sections of the Control of Pollution Act 1974 are brought into effect (see paragraphs 131–133).

II. ADMINISTRATIVE ARRANGEMENTS

General

107. Responsibility for controlling or dealing with marine pollution is divided between several Ministers. The Minister of Agriculture, Fisheries and Food has a general responsibility for safeguarding fishing interests, with a specific responsibility for controlling marine pollution by dumping at sea, with the Secretary of State for Scotland having similar responsibilities in Scotland; the Secretary of State for Trade is responsible for legislation governing the control of oil and chemical pollution, primarily from ships, and for remedial action at sea; the Secretary of State for Energy is responsible for the control of off-shore oil and gas development operations, including the control of pollution from such operations; and the Secretary of State for the Environment has responsibilities in relation to oil and chemicals on beaches in England with the Secretaries of State for Wales and Scotland having these responsibilities in Wales and Scotland.

108. Licences for dredging for sand and gravel are issued by the Crown Estate Commissioners, who first seek the advice of the Department of the Environment (DOE) Hydraulics Research Station (HRS) about the effects of dredging on coastal erosion, and then via the DOE Construction Industry Directorates receive the advice of other Departments about any other possible effect eg on fisheries or shipping.

Dealing with Oil Pollution

109. Government responsibility for action against oil or chemical spills at sea rests with the Department of Trade. Although not statutorily bound to do so, local authorities have accepted the responsibility for clearing oil from beaches, banks of estuaries and up to about one mile from shore. Both central Government and coastal local authorities have emergency organisations to deal quickly with the problem. Oil pollution in docks and harbours is normally dealt with by the dock and harbour authorities concerned. Fishery interests are safeguarded by the Ministry of Agriculture, Fisheries and Food (MAFF) in England and Wales, and by the Department of Agriculture and Fisheries for Scotland (DAFS), and wildlife by the Nature Conservancy Council (NCC).

110. The Department of Trade has an established organisation for reporting spillages of oil which threaten serious coastal pollution or harm to important concentrations of sea birds and for undertaking clearance operations at sea. Standing arrangements exist whereby ships and aircraft report sightings of oil off the coast to HM Coastguard. They in turn inform the appropriate Department of Trade Principal Marine Officer—there are nine of them, each in charge of a marine survey district, which together cover the entire United Kingdom coastline—and, if there is a risk of the oil coming ashore, the local authorities. If clearance action is necessary, and practicable, the Principal Officer concerned will put into effect his contingency arrangements, which have been established for this purpose.

111. Coastal county councils in England and Wales draw up schemes to deal with oil pollution in consultation with the district councils. The county council provides an organisation and resources to support its district councils who do most of the actual cleaning up. In devising schemes the county councils consult the local representatives of MAFF and the NCC. They also consult the Principal Marine Officer of the Department of Trade (DT) for the district, and neighbouring county councils in order to provide for mutual assistance. The scope of schemes extends from dealing with a major spillage to cleaning any minor pollution which occurs. The schemes also provide for the designation of oil pollution officers by the county and district councils. These officers are responsible for the organisation of the local authority arrangements and for the clearance operations. In Scotland regional and islands councils are responsible for the preparation of similar schemes in consultation with district councils, with the DAFS Fishery Inspectorate, and with Principal Officers of DT.

112. Except in very calm waters and in ecologically sensitive areas the most effective way of treating oil on the waters around the United Kingdom is by spraying dispersant on the oil and then agitating the resulting mixture to accelerate the natural process of degradation. The use of dispersants on the sea and foreshore is controlled by the Dumping at Sea Act 1974 (see paragraph 129) and licences for their use are restricted to those which have passed the toxicity test of the MAFF Fisheries Laboratory. Modern dispersants are much less toxic than those used at the time of the Torrey Canyon disaster. Dispersants are also tested for their efficiency by the Department of Industry's Warren Spring Laboratory (SWL). Local authorities are advised periodically by a Newsletter of the dispersants recommended by these two establishments. Oil on beaches is commonly dealt with by physical removal; cleaning up oil pollution can be expensive.

113. The Department of Trade, on behalf of the Government, and the local authorities attempt to recover their clean-up costs whenever those responsible for the pollution can be identified. To date, recovery has most commonly been made from tanker owners in accordance with the Tanker Owners Voluntary

Agreement Concerning Liability for Oil Pollution (TOVALOP) (see paragraph 141). In June 1975, the Merchant Shipping (Oil Pollution) Act 1971, which imposes strict liability for oil pollution on ships carrying cargoes of persistent oil in bulk, came fully into force (see paragraphs 117 and 140). As a general rule, future government claims for clean-up costs against tanker owners will be made by reference to this statute.

Dealing with Pollutants Other Than Oil

114. Similar arrangements have been established for coastal local authorities to deal with containers of chemicals and other substances washed ashore, with the additional need to identify the chemicals involved and to decide how to handle them promptly. Where the object washed ashore is known to be of British manufacture or involves a British trader, the local authority can approach the firm direct or use the "Chemsafe" scheme of the Chemical Industries Association. This scheme provides for a 24 hour enquiry point service for advice and assistance to the emergency services in accidents arising from the movement of hazardous chemical substances. In cases where the item is of foreign origin the "Chemsafe" enquiry point might be able to help but much would depend upon its available resources and experience. In the event of an unknown or un-identified product, local authorities can contact the continuously manned Chemical Emergencies Centre at the Atomic Energy Research Establishment (AERE) Harwell Hazardous Materials service, which may also assist with actual disposal in some areas. In Wales, the Welsh Office has established three panels of experts (on a regional basis) composed of suitably qualified personnel drawn from industry, water authorities and universities. They are available to give help and advice to local authorities in the initial handling of potentially dangerous substances found washed ashore and have the added advantage of providing readily accessible local expertise in the event of an emergency. The Department of Trade plays a part in these arrangements by receiving, and transmitting to all authorities involved, reports of casualties involving dangerous goods and reports of packaged goods reported to be lost overboard or seen floating at sea, and by attempting to identify the shippers involved. Its Principal Marine Officers have also established contacts with the major chemical interests around the coast in order to accumulate a fund of information about the movement of chemicals (including those shipped in bulk) at sea off their districts.

115. IMCO's 1973 Marine Pollution Convention, which is not yet in force (see paragraph 138), makes it mandatory for bulk chemicals to be carried in properly designed and certificated ships, and will result in the better identification of any packaged goods washed ashore. The Convention also makes it compulsory for ships to give notification of any incident at sea involving the release of any dangerous cargoes into the sea, or the loss overboard of any packaged dangerous goods. The United Kingdom is already, with other neighbouring states, in a voluntary notification scheme for hazardous cargoes lost at sea.

34

116. The main statutory provisions to control marine pollution and off-shore operations are as follows:

   (a) Merchant Shipping (Oil Pollution) Act 1971

   (b) Merchant Shipping Act 1974 (Part II)

   (c) Prevention of Oil Pollution Act 1971

   (d) Petroleum (Production) Act 1934

   (e) Mineral Working (Off-shore Installations) Act 1971

   (f) Coast Protection Act 1949

   (g) Continental Shelf Act 1964

   (h) Petroleum and Submarine Pipelines Act 1975

   (i) Dumping at Sea Act 1974

   (j) Sea Fisheries Regulations Act 1966 (England and Wales only)

   (k) Control of Pollution Act 1974.

Merchant Shipping (Oil Pollution) Act 1971

117. The Act places a liability on the owner of a tanker from which oil escapes and requires him to carry insurance against the liability. It has enabled the United Kingdom to ratify the 1969 Civil Liability Convention (see paragraph 140).

Merchant Shipping Act 1974

118. The Merchant Shipping Act 1974 contains provisions about oil pollution from ships and has enabled the United Kingdom to ratify the International Compensation Fund Convention (see paragraph 143). It provides for oil importers to contribute to an international fund that will give compensation for pollution damage in the United Kingdom where persons suffering the damage are unable to obtain full compensation under the Merchant Shipping (Oil Pollution) Act 1971. The Act also enables the Secretary of State to make regulations about the design and construction of British oil tankers and about the admission of foreign tankers to British ports, initially in order to implement the 1971 amendments to the 1954 International Convention for the Prevention of Pollution of the Sea by oil (see paragraph 137). No such regulations have yet been made but British shipowners are voluntarily constructing oil tankers to the standards specified in the 1971 amendments.

Prevention of Oil Pollution Act 1971

119. This Act, inter alia, gives effect to the International Convention for the Prevention of Pollution of the Sea by Oil 1954 as amended in 1962 and again in 1969 (see paragraph 137). It makes it an offence for ships of any nationality to discharge any oil into United Kingdom waters, and additionally for United

Kingdom registered ships to discharge any persistent oil anywhere at sea, except in accordance with very stringent regulations. These discharge requirements are enforced primarily by the Department of Trade and harbour authorities. The Department of Trade follows up reports of illegal discharges at sea and prosecutes alleged offenders whenever it considers it has sufficient evidence and it is practicable to do so. It receives reports from a variety of sources including foreign governments. Such reports are made in accordance with the provisions of the 1954 Convention. The United Kingdom, too, uses these provisions to pass on to other contracting states information received which indicates that their ships may have violated the Convention. The harbour authorities prosecute for offences against the Act which are committed within their port areas. It is hoped that the actions of all prosecuting authorities, and the provision in the Act for the imposition of very heavy fines, have a salutary effect upon those convicted and act as a deterrent to others.

120. The Act introduces into United Kingdom law the provisions of the 1969 Intervention Convention (see paragraph 139) and gives the Secretary of State for Trade the power to intervene in certain circumstances in the event of a shipping casualty, whether occurring on the high seas or in territorial waters, which causes or threatens to cause large scale pollution of our coasts.

121. The Act also controls discharges of oil or oily water from installations on land into United Kingdom waters and from off-shore platforms or pipelines on the United Kingdom continental shelf into the sea. Some exemptions are possible (see paragraph 128). The prevention of accidental pollution from off-shore installations is essentially a matter of using good safe working practices which, whilst aimed primarily at the safety of the men and installations, undoubtedly reduce the risks of pollution from oil spills.

Petroleum (Production) Act 1934

122. Licences to explore for and exploit petroleum oil and gas on the United Kingdom Continental Shelf are issued by the Secretary of State for Energy under powers conferred upon him by section 2(1) of the Petroleum (Production) Act 1934 as applied by section 1(3) of the Continental Shelf Act 1964. The Petroleum (Production) Regulations 1966, made under these Acts as amended by Schedule 2 Part 1 of the Petroleum and Submarine Pipelines Act 1975, set out model clauses which are incorporated in licences. Failure of licensees to abide by the terms and conditions contained in these model clauses renders the licence liable to revocation. The model clauses provide, inter alia, that licence operators must execute their operations in accordance with good oilfield practice. The industry must take steps to confine petroleum won and saved in proper receptacles and to prevent the escape or waste of oil and avoid damage to oil bearing strata.

Mineral Working (Off-shore Installations) Act 1971

123. The operation of off-shore installations is also controlled by the Mineral

Workings (Off-shore Installations) Act 1971, which provides for a comprehensive code of safety, health and welfare regulations. Nine sets of regulations have already been issued and more are to follow. These are not aimed primarily at pollution prevention but, because of the links between safety and the prevention of oil spills, help to reduce the risk of oil pollution. Department of Energy (DEn) Petroleum Production Inspectors ensure that operational activities comply with the regulations and with "Continental Shelf Operations Notices".

Coast Protection Act 1949

124. Precautions are taken to minimise the risk of a collision between a ship and an off-shore installation. Before an installation (whether a mobile drilling platform or a fixed production platform) can be sited, a consent has to be obtained from the Department of Trade under the Coast Protection Act 1949 as extended by the Continental Shelf Act 1964. Navigational requirements are taken into account before a consent is issued. The consents also require installations to be adequately lit and marked and their locations to be publicised in Notices to Mariners and (for fixed installations only) marked on charts. The Convention on the Continental Shelf 1958 allows states to establish safety zones of not more than 500 metres radius around installations, and both British and foreign ships are prohibited from entering safety zones unless they have business with an installation.

Continental Shelf Act 1964

125. The Geneva Convention on the High Seas requires signatories to draw up regulations to prevent pollution of the sea by the discharge of oil from pipelines, and to introduce legislation making the breaking or injury of pipelines an offence. These provisions were put into effect by the Continental Shelf Act 1964, which extended the Submarine Telegraph Act 1885 to include pipelines under the high seas. All pipelines are marked on Admiralty charts warning mariners not to anchor or trawl in the vicinity. Consents for pipelines issued under the 1964 Act also require submarine pipelines to be buried, where practicable, to avoid the risk of damage. Pipelines under the North Sea are given anti-corrosion coatings and for oil lines a special form of impact-resistant concrete has been developed.

126. The Act is also concerned with licences to develop petroleum gas and oil on the United Kingdom Continental Shelf (see paragraph 122), and with the siting of off-shore installations (see paragraph 124).

Petroleum and Submarine Pipelines Act 1975

127. The Petroleum and Submarine Pipelines Act 1975 gives the Secretary of State for Energy powers over the construction, route, capacity, ownership and use of submarine pipelines. In particular it requires the construction and use of submarine pipelines begun after the Act became law to be authorised by the Secretary of State. The Act also empowers the Secretary of State to make

regulations for the safety of pipelines and people working on them, to appoint pipeline inspectors and to hold inquiries into accidents.

128. The Act also makes it possible to grant exemptions from the Prevention of Oil Pollution Act 1971 (see paragraph 121) for certain minimal essential discharges.

Dumping at Sea Act 1974

129. The Dumping at Sea Act 1974 provides the legislative support in the United Kingdom for control of dumping at sea and replaces a previous voluntary control scheme. It provides that before any materials can be disposed of at sea by "dumping" as defined (excluding discharges through pipelines) a certificate must be obtained from the authorising authority, ie MAFF or DAFS. Applications for such licences are made either by the dumping contractor or by those with wastes to be disposed of. The applications are considered by the Departmental authorities against the established criteria for this purpose which are set out in the annexes to the Oslo and London Conventions (see paragraphs 146 and 147). The determining factor in deciding whether to grant a licence is the need to protect the marine environment and its living resources.

Sea Fisheries Regulations Act 1966

130. There is no general control over discharges to the sea from land at present, although Sea Fisheries Committees have power under the Sea Fisheries Regulation Act 1966 (which applies to England and Wales only) to control discharges (except from water authorities' sea outfalls) and dumping in territorial waters of substances harmful to sea fish or sea fisheries. The Sea Fisheries Inspectorate have responsibility for enforcement of this legislation.

Control of Pollution Act 1974

131. The Working Party on Sewage Disposal was set up by the Government to review methods of sewage disposal. Its report published in 1970 included recommendations that discharges to all tidal rivers and estuaries should be fully controlled and that arrangements for the protection of coastal waters should be improved. (There are at present general powers to control only those discharges to tidal rivers and estuaries started after 1960, although specified estuaries and tidal water can be controlled by order (see paragraph 66).) The Royal Commission on Environmental Pollution also made an extensive study of pollution in some British estuaries and coastal waters. Many of the recommendations made by both the Working Party and the Commission have been incorporated in the Control of Pollution Act 1974.

132. The water provisions of the Act, which have not yet been fully implemented, extend previous controls, as described in Chapter 3, to cover discharges of trade and sewage effluents etc to tidal waters or the sea. They will make it an offence for anyone to cause or knowingly permit such a discharge without the consent of the water authority.

133. The Act when fully implemented will enable the United Kingdom to ratify the Convention for the Prevention of Marine Pollution from Land Based Sources which was signed in Paris in June 1974. The Convention relates to the whole of the North Sea and North East Atlantic, including the English Channel.

IV. ADVISORY BODIES

Standing Committee on Pollution Clearance at Sea

134. The Standing Committee on Pollution Clearance at Sea is a joint Government/industry body, chaired by the Department of Trade, which advises the Secretary of State for Trade on measures for clearing up oil pollution.

V. CENTRAL GOVERNMENT ADVICE

135. The main Government circulars issued to local authorities in England and Wales on marine pollution are:

MHLG 54/63	Coastal preservation and development
MHLG 7/66	The coast
MHLG 34/68	Oil pollution of beaches (WO 29/68)
DOE 64/73	Report on survey of discharge of foul sewage to coastal waters (WO 114/73)
DOE 13/74	Oil pollution of beaches (WO 30/74)
DOE 123/74	Emergencies arising from chemicals and other substances washed ashore (WO 201/74)

136. In Scotland, advice has been given in the following main circulars:

SDD 55/68	Oil pollution of beaches
76/74	Emergencies from dangerous substances washed ashore
75/75	Oil pollution of beaches—dangerous substances washed ashore.

VI. INTERNATIONAL ACTION

137. The 1954 International Convention for the Prevention of Pollution of the Sea by Oil, as amended in 1962, limits the intentional discharge of persistent oil within defined zones. These zones extend one hundred miles from most coasts and cover the whole of the North Sea together with a large part of the eastern Atlantic. The 1969 Amendments to the Convention, which are not yet in force internationally, but which the United Kingdom has implemented for its own ships, will replace the prohibited zone system by one prohibiting the discharge of oil in polluting quantities anywhere at sea and prohibiting tankers from discharging any residues from their cargo tanks within 50 miles of land. The 1971 Amendments (again not yet in force) require tankers to comply with specified standards of construction, ie international limitations on the size of individual tanks in the tankers, to reduce the volume of oil that may escape in the event of an accident.

138. The International Convention for the Prevention of Pollution from Ships 1973 has been signed by the United Kingdom but is not yet in force. This consolidates, tightens and improves the 1954 International Convention on the Prevention of Pollution of the Sea by Oil and its various amendments, extends it to non-persistent oils and introduces for the first time regulations restricting the discharge of residues of dangerous chemicals carried in bulk. It also introduces regulations governing the prevention of pollution by harmful packaged substances, sewage and garbage although there is provision for states to adhere to the Convention without excepting these regulations. In certain vulnerable areas or special areas all discharges of these potential pollutants may be prohibited.

139. International action has also been taken to minimise the consequences of any accidents that may happen in spite of these precautions. Two conventions were adopted in 1969 and signed by the United Kingdom, and came into force in 1975. Both have been ratified by the United Kingdom. The first is the International Convention relating to Intervention on the High Seas in Cases of Oil Pollution Casualties 1969 (the "Intervention" Convention); the second the International Convention on Oil Pollution Damage 1969 (the "Civil Liability" Convention). The Intervention Convention recognises the right of coastal states to take protective action to avoid or minimise threatened oil pollution of their coastline in the event of a casualty on the high seas; and lays down procedures for consultation. A protocol covering noxious substances was adopted at the conference and was signed by the United Kingdom in 1973, to extend the Convention to hazardous substances in addition to oil, but is not yet in force.

Liability for Oil Pollution Damage

140. The Civil Liability Convention makes operators of ships carrying 2,000 tons or more of persistent oil in bulk strictly liable for oil pollution damage (with a few exemptions) and requires them to have appropriate insurance to cover this liability. Liability is, however, limited. This convention has been ratified by most states in North West Europe with the result that their tankers and tankers entering their ports must have the stipulated insurance. The Merchant Shipping (Oil Pollution) Act 1971 has enabled the United Kingdom to ratify this convention.

141. Where the Civil Liability Convention does not apply, recompense may be obtained in some cases through a voluntary scheme known as the Tanker Owners Voluntary Agreement Concerning Liability for Oil Pollution (TOVALOP). TOVALOP came into force in October 1969 and provides that when, through negligence of a tanker owner, oil is discharged from a tanker and pollutes or threatens to pollute coastlines the owner must take reasonable steps to prevent and clean up such pollution. The owner is also required to reimburse Governments concerned (including local authorities) for the cost of any clean-up operations up to a maximum of $100 per gross registered ton of the tanker concerned or $10,000,000 whichever is the less.

142. A further voluntary scheme was established in 1971 which supplements both TOVALOP and the Civil Liability Convention. It provides compensation for situations where there is shipowner's exemption or compensation is insufficient. The scheme is known as the Contract Regarding an Interim Supplement to Tanker Liability for Oil Pollution (CRISTAL). The maximum compensation available per incident is $30,000,000. An oil company which becomes a party to CRISTAL makes a periodic payment to a central fund, derived by assessing the crude oil and fuel oil receipts for the previous year.

143. The International Convention on the Establishment of an International Fund for Compensation for Oil Pollution Damage 1971 has been adopted, signed and ratified by the United Kingdom but is not yet in force. It will replace the voluntary CRISTAL scheme.

144. An oil spillage from an off-shore operation in an area under another state's jurisdiction could affect the United Kingdom and vice versa: for this reason the question of civil liability for oil pollution damage from off-shore operations is appropriately tackled on a North West European regional basis. An intergovernmental working party has drafted a text of a convention and, with the object of adopting it, the United Kingdom hosted a diplomatic conference in London in October 1975 which was adjourned to December 1976.

145. As an interim measure the British off-shore oil industry has devised a voluntary off-shore pollution liability agreement (OPOL). This came into force on 1 May 1975, and provides up to $25,000,000 per incident to compensate for oil pollution damage caused by the operations of members of the agreement, other than movement of tankers. The scheme is similar in concept and effect to both TOVALOP and CRISTAL. The scheme has since been extended to any operators from Denmark, the Federal Republic of Germany, France, Ireland, the Netherlands and Norway who may wish to join.

Dumping at Sea

146. Dumping at sea is subject to various international controls. The Oslo Convention to control dumping in the North East Atlantic area (which includes all seas around the United Kingdom) was signed in 1972, came into force on 7 April 1974 and was ratified by the United Kingdom on 30 June 1975. The London Convention—of global effect—was signed in London in 1972 and came into effect in August 1975; the United Kingdom, which ratified the Convention in November 1975, is a depository Government. It provided the interim secretariat for the Consultative meeting of the Contracting Parties in December 1975 which nominated IMCO as the Secretariat. The Commission of the EEC have recently published a draft directive which would in its draft form affect the detailed control of dumping in the sea, exercised at present under the Oslo and London Conventions.

147. The Conventions require all dumping to be authorised by national authorities and restrict the dumping of potentially harmful wastes. Both

Conventions contain a list (Annex I) of families of substances which may not be dumped, apart from those members of the families which are non-toxic or rapidly converted in the sea into substances which are biologically harmless. These substances remain subject to the provisions of Annexes II and III. Annex II contains certain other listed substances in disposing of which special care must be taken: before disposal the substances concerned should be considered in relation to their toxicity, persistence, solubility and biodegradability, and the areas for disposal are selected to ensure suitable dilution and dispersal and to avoid harm to marine resources.

Other International Aspects

148. Other conventions related to marine pollution are the Convention on the Continental Shelf 1958 (paragraph 124), the Geneva Convention on the High Seas (paragraph 125), and the Convention for the Prevention of Marine Pollution from Land Based Sources 1974 (paragraph 133). The United Kingdom is also a contracting party to the Agreement for Co-operation in dealing with Pollution of the North Sea by Oil. Under this agreement, known as the "Bonn Agreement", the eight states bordering the North Sea have agreed to assist each other by reporting the presence and movement of oil spills which might threaten each other's coasts, to provide additional resources for dealing with major incidents, and to exchange information about their contingency arrangements and about new measures for dealing with oil pollution.

149. The United Nations Conference on the Law of the Sea is drafting a chapter on the preservation of the marine environment as part of a comprehensive Law of the Sea Convention.

VII. MONITORING

150. A survey of the discharges of foul sewage to the coastal waters of England and Wales was made in 1972 and a report published in 1973. At that time 149 coastal local authorities and seven sewerage boards discharged sewage to the sea through 330 outfalls. No treatment was given to the discharges from 198 of these outfalls. The survey is now being updated.

151. Monitoring is an essential part of pollution control arrangements for the sea, both to establish the current situation and to maintain a check over changes taking place as a result of authorised and unauthorised waste disposal activities. MAFF and DAFS Fisheries Laboratories are responsible for monitoring various pollutants in water, mud, silt, fish and shellfish, and the Natural Environment Research Council (NERC) and the Laboratory of the Government Chemist record levels of pesticide residues and polychlorinated biphenyls in seabirds as well as carrying out other studies on the marine environment.

152. MAFF and DAFS Fisheries Laboratories play a full part in the International Council for the Exploration of the Sea (ICES) where an extended programme of baseline monitoring over the whole of the North Atlantic has

recently been agreed. The parties to the Oslo and Paris Conventions have agreed to set up monitoring schemes in which ICES will play a part.

153. In parallel with this activity the Marine Pollution Monitoring Management Group has been set up under MAFF chairmanship to report to the Central Unit on Environmental Pollution as one of the six monitoring management groups referred to in Chapter 1. The objective of the Group is to provide the overall strategy for marine pollution monitoring in the context of nationwide and international obligations and to carry the work forward in harmony with the other five monitoring management groups.

VIII. RESEARCH

154. Research into new methods of clearing oil and the approval of materials and items of equipment for use on the sea and shore is carried out by Warren Spring Laboratory. Their findings are conveyed to coastal local authorities and other interested bodies by a Newsletter issued each year or by special publications prepared by the Laboratory. Research on booms, which float on the water surface and contain the spread of oil, is also conducted by the Hydraulics Research Station. This station advises on the different types of boom available and the techniques for using them. The MAFF Fisheries Laboratory tests dispersants for their toxicity and carries out research on the toxity of oil itself. In connection with the development of off-shore oil production, the Department of Energy is funding a programme of research into oil/water separation techniques and into systems of monitoring oily water discharges arising from production operations.

155. Research on the behaviour and effects of pollutants reaching the sea through discharges and from rivers is carried out by laboratories of MAFF and DAFS and is supported by the Institute for Marine Environmental Research and elsewhere by NERC. Persistent pollutants such as heavy metals and organochlorine compounds receive particular attention.

CHAPTER 5

WASTE DISPOSAL

I. INTRODUCTION

156. The Government's approach to waste management is based on the principle that the primary task for local and central Government is to ensure that satisfactory means of waste disposal are provided for all wastes arising in the country. These bodies should ensure that pollution of air, water or land is avoided so far as possible in the disposal of wastes; that wastes are disposed of safely without risk to employees and the public; that nuisance or inconvenience to the public from waste disposal operations is minimised, and that the reclamation and re-use of materials and the use of waste materials for positive ends such as land reclamation or heat generation is encouraged.

157. The present role of local authorities in England and Wales has developed from the Public Health Acts of 1875 and 1936 which gave them certain powers and duties in respect of refuse collection and disposal. However, the Public Health Acts mention waste disposal only briefly amongst many other matters and they have little or nothing to say about industrial waste. In Scotland the majority of local authorities are still exercising refuse collection and disposal functions under the Burgh Police (Scotland) Acts 1892–1903, which make no special provisions for trade and industrial waste. These measures are not adequate for a situation in which the disposal of industrial waste, particularly toxic substances, is giving rise to increasing concern and in which the inadequacy of a fragmented and unco-ordinated approach to waste disposal has become increasingly apparent.

158. Growing concern in the 1960s about the environmental effects of waste led to the setting up of two Working Groups, one on the Disposal of Solid Toxic Wastes (in 1964) and one on Refuse Disposal in general (in 1967). Those groups made the most detailed investigations yet into waste disposal in this country and identified a number of major failings. These were:

(a) the lack of any machinery or responsibility for strategic planning of waste disposal over wide areas;

(b) the poor siting and offensive operation of certain waste disposal facilities so as to damage amenity;

(c) the danger of pollution, for example of water supplies, by abandoned wastes, especially toxic industrial wastes;

(d) the failure to take full advantage of the best modern technology, of opportunities for integration of waste disposal facilities, and of possibilities for recycling materials and reclaiming land;

(e) the need for more research.

159. The two reports concluded that there needed to be more public control over the whole process of waste disposal to ensure that it was carried out safely and inoffensively, taking full advantage of modern technology, and was well integrated with land-use planning and other environmental requirements. The reports also recommended that this control should be carried out by local authorities, given the existing role of local authorities in waste collection and disposal.

II. ADMINISTRATIVE ARRANGEMENTS

post 1974 Local Government Re-organisation

160. Responsibility for the collection of domestic and trade waste in England and Wales lies with the new district authorities, who are also responsbile for the disposal of bulky refuse, and street cleansing. In England the new county authorities are responsible for waste disposal, including the operation of incinerators and tips, but in Wales disposal is carried out by the new district councils. In Scotland both waste collection and disposal functions are carried out by district councils and islands councils. Industrial wastes are generally dealt with by private enterprise. Local authorities in England and Wales are advised on their duties by means of circulars by the Department of the Environment (DOE) and the Welsh Office (WO) who have, in addition, initiated a series of visits to local authorities for discussions about their needs and problems. Local authorities in Scotland are advised by the Scottish Development Department (SDD).

161. Most ordinary household refuse and much of the waste arising from trade and commercial premises are under the control of local authorities. Farm wastes, mining and quarrying wastes and industrial wastes are less closely controlled. Farm wastes are mostly disposed of according to good agricultural practice and the Ministry of Agriculture, Fisheries and Food (MAFF) and the Department of Agriculture and Fisheries for Scotland (DAFS) actively promote these practices through their advisory services. Mining and quarrying wastes are controlled to a large extent by planning consents for exploitation. Industrial (as well as domestic and commercial) wastes will be subject to control under the Control of Pollution Act and work is already under way within DOE to determine the best practicable means of disposal for the most significant toxic and hazardous wastes, the disposal of which is at present subject to control under the Deposit of Poisonous Waste Act 1972.

162. The Government issued a Green Paper, "War on Waste", in 1974 which contained a policy for reclamation. Local authorities are being encouraged to consider various aspects of reclamation and recycling both now and within the framework of future powers and duties under the Control of Pollution Act 1974. Such measures include separate collection of particular wastes for recovery, establishment of reclamation centres, possible arrangements for separating some types of waste, and the form in which wastes could best be used, not only as material for industry, but as a source of heat or electricity or as infill in land reclamation schemes. In particular authorities have been

urged by the Government to consider the possibility of setting up waste paper collection services if they have not already done so and to encourage more collection of various materials by private dealers or voluntary organisations.

III. LEGISLATION

163. The statutory provisions which affect waste disposal are as follows:

    (a) Public Health Act 1936

    (b) Burgh Police (Scotland) Acts 1892–1903

    (c) Civic Amenities Act 1967

    (d) Litter Act 1958 and Dangerous Litter Act 1971

    (e) Local Government (Development and Finance) (Scotland) Act 1964

    (f) Deposit of Poisonous Waste Act 1972

    (g) Control of Pollution Act 1974

    (h) Health and Safety at Work etc Act 1974.

Public Health Act 1936

164. At present the legal provisions governing the collection and disposal of household and trade refuse in England and Wales are contained in the Public Health Act 1936. This Act provides local authorities with enabling powers to collect and dispose of household waste free of charge and a power to collect waste from trade premises (shops, offices etc) on payment. Although these powers are discretionary (subject to a power of direction by the Secretary of State), in practice local authorities invariably use them. Some local authorities make special arrangements for salvaging waste paper.

165. The same Act also enables local authorities to sell refuse removed by them and to provide:—

    (a) receptacles for refuse in streets and public places;

    (b) places for the deposit of refuse; and

    (c) plant or apparatus for treating or disposing of refuse.

166. These provisions have largely been concerned with providing a basic but rather limited legal framework for the collection and disposal of this sort of waste. Local authorities are also given powers to empty cesspools and privies and to sweep and water streets.

Burgh Police (Scotland) Acts 1892–1903

167. In Scotland the functions of collection and disposal of waste are exercised by district and islands councils under the provisions of the Burgh Police (Scotland) Acts 1892–1903 or a local Act, or a combination of these according to the part of the district or islands area concerned and its previous legislative background. In the areas where they apply the Burgh Police Acts provide local authorities with powers to collect and dispose of domestic refuse, to clean

46

streets, to provide places for the disposal of rubbish and to provide vehicles, buildings, machinery and plant to facilitate disposal. No present powers exist, other than in local Acts, for the collection of trade or industrial waste.

Civic Amenities Act 1967

168. This Act provides, among other things, for the orderly disposal of disused vehicles and other bulky refuse. Under this Act local authorities are obliged to provide places where residents may conveniently and free of charge deposit refuse (other than business refuse). At the same time the Act makes it an offence to abandon a motor vehicle or other rubbish on open land or a highway. When rubbish is abandoned in the open air, local authorities have power to remove it, subject to a right of objection by the occupier of the land. But they are under an obligation to remove abandoned vehicles from open land and highways.

Litter Act 1958 and Dangerous Litter Act 1971

169. The depositing of litter in public places was made an offence attracting a fine of up to £10 by the Litter Act 1958. The Dangerous Litter Act 1971 increased the maximum fine to £100 and required the courts, in sentencing convicted persons, to have regard to any risk of injury to persons or animals.

Local Government (Development and Finance) (Scotland) Act 1964

170. This Act gives district and islands councils in Scotland powers to provide and maintain litter bins and to collect and dispose of litter in certain places.

Deposit of Poisonous Waste Act 1972

171. Industrial wastes were not covered by any legislation until the Deposit of Poisonous Waste Act was passed in 1972 following public concern about the indiscriminate dumping of toxic industrial waste. Under Section 1 of the Act it is an offence punishable by heavy penalties (a maximum of £400 and/or 6 months' imprisonment on summary conviction and 5 years' imprisonment and/ or an unlimited fine on indictment) to deposit on land any poisonous, noxious or polluting waste in circumstances in which it can cause danger to persons or animals or pollute water supplies. This does not seek to eliminate disposal to land but rather to instil a sense of responsibility in those concerned with waste disposal, so that adequate precautions are taken at suitable sites and disposal at unsuitable sites in previous use is discontinued.

172. The Act requires those removing or disposing of certain types of waste to notify the waste disposal authority and the regional water authority at least three clear working days before they do so, giving details of the composition, quantity and destination of the waste. Since the passage of the Act local authorities have had information available on the arising and deposit of wastes in their area and have been able to advise firms disposing of wastes where particular problems are likely to occur.

173. Also in this Act are requirements for landfill site operators to give similar confirmation within three clear working days of disposal. The wastes concerned in this notification system are those not specifically excluded as unlikely to be poisonous, noxious or polluting by regulations issued in July 1972. This is not, of course, a consent procedure but provides local and water authorities (in Scotland, river purification authorities) with knowledge of the nature and quantities of such wastes in their areas and also enables them to consider how far there might be risks of any offence being committed under section 1 of the Act. The Act covers England, Scotland and Wales. The offence provisions have been in operation since 30 March 1972 and the notification procedure since 3 August 1972.

Control of Pollution Act 1974

174. Part I of the Control of Pollution Act deals with waste on land and provides for the implementation of many of the recommendations of the Working Groups on the Disposal of Solid Toxic Waste and Refuse Disposal. Due to the current economic circumstances implementation of many of the major provisions of the Act has been deferred, although those dealing with the reclamation of waste were brought into force in January 1976 in England and Wales and the provisions on site licensing were brought into effect on 14 June 1976. The Act provides the statutory framework for a systematic and co-ordinated approach to waste collection and disposal. When sections 1 and 2 of the Act are implemented waste disposal authorities will be required to carry out a survey of the wastes requiring disposal in their areas and to prepare plans to ensure that satisfactory facilities are available, whether in the public or private sector, for the receipt of household, commercial and industrial waste.

175. The primary method of establishing control over waste disposal operations will be by means of a site licensing system, whereby all persons wishing to operate disposal sites or treatment plants will be required to seek a site licence from the waste disposal authority. It will be an offence for any person to deposit controlled waste on land or to use plant or equipment to dispose of controlled waste unless there is a licence issued by the waste disposal authority and its conditions are complied with. Penalties of up to £400 on summary conviction and a maximum of two years in prison or a fine or both on indictment are provided in the Act for unlicensed dumping. The waste disposal authorities will be able to impose operating conditions on the sites and will have extensive supervisory and enforcement powers to ensure that sites are run satisfactorily and that the conditions of operation are met. Waste disposal authorities will be required to ensure that similar standards are maintained at their own sites.

176. In addition to the disposal provisions the Act will provide redefined duties and powers for local authorities in respect of the collection of waste. It broadens the sphere of the local authority responsibility, established under earlier legislation, for the collection and disposal of refuse, by requiring collection authorities to collect all household waste free of charge except in certain prescribed cir-

cumstances; to collect all commercial waste on request, and to make a charge unless the authority considers it inappropriate to do so.

177. The Act provides powers for both disposal and collection authorities to collect industrial waste, though in this case a charge must be made. It is not, however, intended that the local authorities should compete with the private sector service for the disposal of industrial waste. The private sector plays a very valuable role in waste disposal and provides services that local authorities could not offer at present and which in any case it might not be suitable for them to offer.

178. The Government have taken the view that a more intensive control mechanism is necessary in relation to specially hazardous and difficult waste. Sites receiving such "special" wastes will be subject to especially stringent operating conditions and, in addition, it is intended to impose controls on the producers. The details of these controls are to be developed in regulations. At present working groups comprising government officials and representatives of waste disposal authorities and of industry are analysing the main groups of industrial waste which might fall into this category and will be making recommendations about the best methods of handling and disposal and any need for special care. These recommendations will be incorporated in technical memoranda which will provide advice and guidance on the proper handling and disposal of the "special waste" in question so that both producers and site operators can take suitable advance precautions. In addition the memoranda will assist waste disposal authorities in producing the type of operating conditions that will need to be attached to sites receiving "special wastes".

179. Heavy penalties are provided for offences against the regulations and in particular stringent provisions are available in the Act to deal with dumping of hazardous waste in a way that could cause an environmental hazard, ie in circumstances in which it might cause danger to persons or animals or might pollute any water supply. The offence provision follows closely the one already in operation under the Deposit of Poisonous Waste Act 1972, which was intended as an interim measure pending the new legislation now introduced. Once the relevant sections of Part I of the 1974 Act are implemented and regulations introduced the Deposit of Poisonous Waste Act 1972 will be repealed.

180. Increasing attention is being paid to the need to conserve resources and recycle waste materials wherever this is practicable and economic. A number of provisions relating to reclamation contained in the Control of Pollution Act 1974 have been implemented in England and Wales (see also paragraph 163 above). In particular:

(a) section 2(4) of Part I of the Act requires waste disposal authorities to consider the possibilities for reclamation of wastes in their areas as part of the preparation of their waste disposal plans;

(b) section 20 gives disposal authorities powers to carry out schemes for reclaiming and re-using waste materials and this would include the provision of plant and equipment. The provision enabling local authorities to buy and sell waste does not mean that it is intended that they should set up in competition with the reclamation industries but rather that local authorities should be able to make use of those waste materials that would not normally be acceptable to commercial firms or come their way. Section 14 of the Act (which does not apply to Scotland) requires collection authorities to deliver for disposal all the waste they collect (except waste paper or other waste materials for recycling) and enables them to provide plant and equipment for the sorting and baling of the waste paper or for the processing of other waste for re-use;

(c) section 21 gives disposal authorities powers to use their waste for the purpose of producing heat or electricity, subject to certain conditions.

Health and Safety at Work etc Atc 1974

181. This Act requires that waste be disposed of without risk to employees or to the public.

IV. ADVISORY BODIES

182. The Waste Management Advisory Council was established in December 1974 and is chaired jointly by Ministers from the DOE and Department of Industry (DI). Its terms of reference are: "To keep under review the development of waste management policies in the United Kingdom having regard to the need to secure the best use of resources, and the safe and efficient disposal of wastes; to give particular consideration to ways of reclaiming materials from waste, recycling materials from waste, recycling techniques, the inter-relationship of waste utilisation and waste disposal, and the reduction or transformation of waste arising; to consider the technical, economic, administrative and legal problems involved; to consider the programme of research and development; and to make recommendations".

183. The range of studies suggested by these terms was very wide but the Green Paper, "War on Waste", published in 1974 made it clear that the Council's primary objective was to provide machinery for a detailed and wide ranging study of the possibilities of reducing waste and of increasing waste reclaimed for re-use or recycling. In selecting priorities the Council has adopted as criteria the prospects of useful returns and the degree of public concern in regard to them. The broader issues being examined include economic obstacles to reclamation and the circumstances in which Government intervention might be appropriate; current research and development and its possible augmentation; and the ways in which the co-operation of industry, local authorities, voluntary organisations and the public might best be obtained. Studies on packaging ferrous metals and non-ferrous metals represent the first of a series on the narrower issues. The Council's first report was published in January 1976.

V. CENTRAL GOVERNMENT ADVICE

184. The main Government circulars issued to local authorities on waste are:

MHLG	44/58	The Litter Act 1958 (SHD 9273)
	31/59	Litter
	52/59	Litter bins
	15/60	Litter
	20/61	Pollution of water by tipped refuse
SDD	38/64	Local Government (Development and Finance) (Scotland) Act 1964
MHLG	8/65	Disposal of old motor vehicles (WO 8/65)
	34/67	Report of the Working Group on Refuse Collection (WO 65/67, SDD letter May 1967)
	55/67	Civic Amenities Act 1967: Part III (WO 49/67, SDD 56/67)
SDD	29/68	Removal of Refuse (Scotland) Regulations 1967
MHLG	80/69	Disposal of asbestos waste (WO 81/69, SDD 75/69)
	69/70	Report of the Technical Committee on the Disposal of Solid Toxic Wastes (WO 87/70, SDD 86/70)
	77/70	Safe disposal of disused refrigerators (WO 98/70, SDD 103/70)
DOE	26/71	Report of the Working Party on Refuse Disposal (WO 65/71, SDD 27/71)
	42/71	Dangerous Litter Act 1971 (WO 42/71, SDD 93/71)
	70/72	Deposit of Poisonous Waste Act 1972 (WO 70/72, SDD 67/72)
	37/72	Review of waste disposal facilities (WO 86/72)
	131/72	Local Government Act 1972: Sections 101 and 110 Arrangements for the discharge of functions ("Agency Arrangements") (WO 227/72)
	55/73	First Report of the Standing Committee on Research into Refuse Collections, Storage and Disposal (WO 128/73, SDD Letter May 73)
	101/74	Report of Working Group on Disposal of Awkward Household Wastes (WO 167/74, SDD 35/74)
	140/74	Green Paper "War on Waste—a Policy for Reclamation" Cmnd 5727 (WO 224/74, SDD 63/74)
SDD	53/75	Local Government (Scotland) Act 1973—Refuse Collection and Disposal
	97/75	Waste collection and disposal and litter—Departmental Circulars
DOE	1/76	Control of Pollution Act 1974—Part I (Waste on Land) Commencement Order No. 4 (WO 1/76)
	3/76	Waste Management Papers (WO 4/76)
	39/76	The balancing of interests between water protection and waste disposal (WO 53/76)

DOE   55/76   Control of Pollution Act 1974—Part I (Waste on Land)
Disposal Licences
63/76   Dustbin hire charges (WO 71/76).

VI. INTERNATIONAL ACTION

185. The main international agreements affecting disposal of waste on land are those proposed by the EEC, which is in the course of issuing a number of directives on this subject. Two directives have been adopted which cover wastes in general and waste oils and are intended to protect human health and the environment by reducing pollution and to encourage recycling within the Community. A draft directive on toxic wastes is in preparation, and directives on wastes from agriculture, and from quarrying and mining, are expected.

186. The European Commission is also carrying out studies on wastes or residues especially harmful to the environment, disposal or re-use of slaughter-house waste, the creation of tips for wastes from surface treatment of metals, and composting, amongst others.

VII. MONITORING

187. DOE has established a Land Pollution Monitoring Management group (see paragraph 12) to consider the problems involved in monitoring pollution on land, including aspects of deliberate or accidental dumping of potentially hazardous waste substances and intentional spreading of materials for industrial or agricultural purposes, as well as the effect of pollution on land use planning. This group will work in harmony with the other five Monitoring Management Groups.

VIII. RESEARCH

188. Government Departments support wide-ranging research programmes covering many aspects of waste management, and substantial experience and facilities are available at several major Government research establishments. Much research on waste treatment and recovery is conducted at the Department of Industry (DI) Warren Spring Laboratory (WSL), mainly sponsored by DOE; and the Atomic Energy Research Establishment (AERE) at Harwell has a Hazardous Materials Service. This carries out research into the treatment of hazardous waste and advises local authorities, industry etc on the best methods of waste disposal and treatment.

CHAPTER 6

RADIOACTIVITY

I. INTRODUCTION

189. The exposure of man to ionising radiations can be increased through the testing of nuclear weapons; through emission from places where radioactive materials are used, such as power stations or hospitals, or from radioactive material in transit; or through the disposal of waste radioactive matter in solid, liquid or gaseous form. This chapter deals with the last two aspects which have been kept under close watch since the expanded programme of nuclear research and development was embarked upon shortly after the end of the 1939–45 war.

190. Radioactive substances are used in nuclear power stations, hospitals, universities and industry. Design and use of equipment using radioactive substances is subject to strict controls under the Nuclear Installations Act 1965 and the Health and Safety at Work etc Act 1974 to reduce any risk of accidental escape of radiation or radioactive material. Control of radioactive waste is more complex. When the United Kingdom Atomic Energy Authority (UKAEA) was formed in 1954 it was recognised that the existing body of law under which the environment was protected against pollution was inadequate to control the radioactive wastes arising from the programme. The disposal of radioactive waste, except that produced by the major users, was subject only to the law governing normal waste disposal. This control was often capable of being invoked or enforced only after a discharge was made and the methods of control were not well suited to a hazard so difficult to detect and so far-reaching in its effects.

Panel to Advise on Radioactive Waste

191. In June 1956 the Radioactive Substance Advisory Committee (set up under the Radioactive Substances Act 1948—see paragraph 203 below) accordingly set up a Panel to advise on the problems of radioactive waste. The terms of reference of this Panel included the need to make an assessment of the amount of waste likely to arise in the future; they were to give advice on the best method of disposal and on whether new legislation or amendments to existing legislation were necessary to ensure safe disposal and, if so, to advise on the form which the new provisions or amendments should take.

192. The Panel reported in March 1958 and the report was published as the White Paper "The Control of Radioactive Wastes" (Cmnd 884) in November 1959. The Panel was firmly of the opinion that control should be exercised at national level, since radioactive wastes could, conceivably, by their genetic effect, affect the whole country; and because it would be best to concentrate the necessary highly trained staff in a centralised body. The Panel recommended

a national disposal service to deal with highly active waste, although local disposal of waste was desirable where possible, both to provide dilution in the environment and to avoid increased exposure due to multiple handling.

193. The Panel considered that future legislation would be needed, to help shape a national policy. The objectives of the policy would be to ensure that radioactive waste arisings were kept to a minimum and that their disposal would not cause any hazard either to the general public or the environment, and are summarised as follows:

(a) to ensure, irrespective of cost, that exposure of individual members of the public is within dose limits recommended by the UN International Commission on Radiological Protection (ICRP), and, on average over the whole population of the country, is within a limit of 1 rem per person in 30 years;

(b) to do what is reasonably practicable, having due regard to cost, convenience and the national importance of this subject, to reduce the doses far below these levels.

194. The Government accepted the Panel's recommendations and Parliament gave effect to them in the Radioactive Substances Act 1960.

195. It is not possible to lay down hard and fast rules for the disposal of radioactive wastes. Each case is treated on its merits by the Radiochemical Inspectorate when making recommendations to the Secretaries of State for the Environment and for Wales. Broadly, the recommendations of the ICRP and the Medical Research Council (MRC) are used to assess the hazards of a discharge. Certain factors have to be watched. For example, when disposals are made to a local authority tip for controlled burial, it must provide adequate cover. There should be no possibility of contaminating local drinking water supplies, and if the wastes are long-lived the possibility of their being disturbed must be assessed. Liquid waste disposals to a sewer necessitate an assessment of the dilution suffered and a knowledge of any processes to which the sewage may be subjected. Discharges of gaseous waste require a knowledge of the concentration of activity in the plume and an assessment as to whether this constitutes a hazard to anyone. Furthermore discharges of liquid effluent via pipeline into the open sea or estuaries, or specified streams and rivers, require an assessment of the effects on fish and plant life, as well as hazards to people. In addition nearly all discharges have some special problem which needs to be taken into consideration.

196. After consideration of all these points the majority of radioactive discharges are many orders of magnitude below levels which would give rise to doses above the level regarded as acceptable by the ICRP or the MRC. This is true of individual discharges and there is little cumulative effect. Considerations of safety are paramount in the granting of authorisations for discharges under the Radioactive Substances Act 1960; at present it is possible to authorise all

necessary discharges without approaching the point at which public safety would be put at risk.

197. Irradiated fuel is reprocessed by British Nuclear Fuels Limited at Windscale and the fissile material is recovered for re-use. The resultant highly active wastes (liquid and solid) are stored in such a way as to isolate them from the environment. Many of these wastes are very long-lived and will remain hazardous for hundreds of years; at present there is no alternative to storage until means of safe disposal have been developed. The low activity wastes are discharged to the environment under the authorisation procedures described in paragraphs 207–221 below.

II. ADMINISTRATIVE ARRANGEMENTS

198. Responsibilities for radioactive materials are spread between a number of Government Departments and agencies. Responsibility for the design and operation of nuclear power stations and of waste treatment and storage facilities lies ultimately with the Secretary of State for Energy. The UKAEA and the Central Electricity Generating Board (CEGB) are his agent authorities for the design and construction of power stations; the waste fuel treatment plant at Windscale and the radioactive waste storage facility at Drigg are operated by BNFL.

199. The Secretary of State for Energy does not have a day to day responsibility for nuclear health and safety. This lies with the Health and Safety Commission under the Health and Safety at Work etc Act 1974, and the Health and Safety Executive (HSE), who report to the Secretary of State for Energy in respect of this function. HSE control the Nuclear Installations Inspectorate (NII) and are responsible for the day to day work of determining safety standards; for ensuring that they are complied with; and for promoting safety—assessing the acceptability of existing standards and the measures necessary to prevent injury and damage, whether from nuclear accidents or from radioactivity emitted in the normal course of operation. HSE are also responsible for the licensing and inspection of nuclear installations, apart from those operated by the UKAEA.

200. The disposal of nuclear wastes, including material discharged directly to the environment by power stations and treatment plant, is the responsibility of the Secretaries of State for the Environment, for Wales and for Scotland in the case of major nuclear establishments, in conjunction with the Minister of Agriculture, Fisheries and Food. High-level wastes are stored rather than disposed of. The Secretary of State for Energy is responsible for approving plans for the siting of new power stations, and the Secretary of State for Transport for the regulations controlling the transport of radioactive materials including wastes. The environmental effects from any proposed nuclear power station and the methods of limiting them are discussed with the operators, the HSE, DOE (or WO) and the Ministry of Agriculture, Fisheries and Food (MAFF) at an early stage of design.

201. This practice extends in effect to all major nuclear installations. Both DOE/WO and MAFF have an interest in all forms of discharge to the environment in the case of major installations, although the Department primarily affected varies with the specific discharges concerned. The Radiochemical Inspectorate (who report to the Secretaries of State for the Environment and for Wales) cover all aspects of radioactive discharges, while within MAFF the technical and scientific support is provided by the Fisheries Radiobiological Laboratory (FRL) and the Atomic Energy Branch covering the marine food and agricultural interests respectively. The Alkali Inspectorate provides additional technical advice on discharges to the atmosphere and the means of reducing them. Small users are controlled by the Radiochemical Inspectorate. The Secretary of State for Wales (together with MAFF in the case of major establishments) is responsible for wastes in the Principality but is advised by the Radiochemical Inspectorate; HM Industrial Pollution Inspectorate (HMIPI), which is a completely separate Inspectorate, is responsible to the Secretary of State for Scotland.

III. LEGISLATION

202. The main legislation affecting the control of radioactive substances is as follows:

(a) Radioactive Substances Acts 1948 and 1960

(b) Atomic Energy Authority Acts 1954 and 1971 and Nuclear Installations (Licensing and Insurance) Act 1959

(c) Nuclear Installations Acts 1965 and 1969

(d) Radiological Protection Act 1970

(e) Health and Safety at Work etc Act 1974.

Radioactive Substances Act 1948

203. The Radioactive Substances Act 1948 made provision for the control of imports and exports of active substances, the use of therapeutic irradiating apparatus, the formulation of safety regulations and the setting up of an Advisory Committee to advise the appropriate Minister on any matters arising under the Act. That part of the Act relating to safety regulations specifically included the disposal of wastes. However, apart from the establishment of the Advisory Committee, the Act required that action be taken by regulation and in the case of that part of the Act relating to safety regulations the appropriate Minister was not named; he was to be designated by Order in Council. Since most of the provisions of the Act specified that the appropriate Minister should consult with the Advisory Committee before making any regulations under the Act, the setting up of this Committee was the first, and for some time the only, provision of the Act to be implemented.

204. For administrative reasons connected with the issue by the then Ministry of Labour of a Code of Practice for workers in research laboratories, an Order

56

in Council made in 1964, SI 699, named the then Minister of Labour as the appropriate Minister. The Secretary of State for the Environment has also been named as the appropriate Minister and has made regulations under the Act: the Radioactive Substances (Carriage by Road) (Great Britain) Regulations 1974 and the Radioactive Substances (Road Transport Workers) (Great Britain) Regulations 1970 and 1975. These regulations ensure that packages used to transport radioactive material are designed to be safe in transit. Different types of packaging are specified for wastes of different levels of radioactivity and packages for higher level wastes are especially stringently designed to be safe even under severe accident conditions, including fire.

Atomic Energy Authority Act 1954

205. This Act established the UKAEA and also made some provision to control radioactive wastes. The UKAEA was only allowed to discharge radioactive waste from its premises with the authorisation of the Minister of Housing and Local Government (now the Secretary of State for the Environment) and the Minister of Agriculture, Fisheries and Food. These discharges were removed from control by local bodies so far as their radioactivity was concerned: but before giving authorisations the Ministers were to consult with such local authorities, water boards, local fisheries committees or other public or local authorities as appeared proper to be consulted. Later under the Nuclear Installations (Licensing and Insurance) Act 1959 the same controls were applied to licensed nuclear sites such as nuclear power stations.

206. The Atomic Energy Authority Act 1971 established the BNFL and the Radiochemical Centre as public bodies. These had previously been part of the UKAEA.

Radioactive Substances Act 1960

207. The Act came into effect on 1 December 1963, the day following that on which powers to control wastes under the Atomic Energy Authority Act 1954 expired. It is concerned mainly with the safe disposal of wastes rather than their treatment and storage, so it affects mainly low-level nuclear wastes. The Act gives permanent effect, in substantially the same form, to the temporary controls to which the discharge of waste by the UKAEA and nuclear site licensees was subject by virtue of the 1954 and 1959 Acts.

208. Authorisations must be given for the disposal of radioactive wastes from UKAEA premises and licensed nuclear sites in England by both the Secretary of State for the Environment and the Minister of Agriculture, Fisheries and Food; in Wales by both the Secretary of State for Wales and the Minister of Agriculture, Fisheries and Food; in Scotland by the Secretary of State for Scotland. Each Minister must consult such local and public authorities as he considers proper.

209. All other users, except Crown establishments, must register in respect of their premises with the Secretary of State for the Environment in England, or

the appropriate Secretary of State in Wales and Scotland. Although Crown establishments are exempt from the provisions of the Act, controls similar to those exercised over other premises are exercised by administrative means. Hospitals managed by Area Health Authorities are exempt from the need to register, but not from the other provisions of the Act.

210. The reason for registration is that proper control of radioactive waste must entail some control at source, so that users who are likely to create a waste hazard by their method of use can be checked before the waste arises. Exemption from registration is given in certain cases where an equivalent control already exists or where the amount of radioactive material is too small to justify registration. Apart from certain exemptions in the Act, the Act also empowers Ministers to grant further exemptions by order, and several such orders have been made. Users of radioactive materials are in no way absolved from responsibility because the material is covered by an Exemption Order. The Secretary of State may attach such conditions to an Order as he thinks fit.

211. In granting registration in respect of premises the Secretary of State may impose certain conditions, but apart from conditions relating to the removal of radioactive material from the premises or the labelling of radioactive material these must have regard solely to the amount or nature of the radioactive waste likely to arise.

212. Registration in respect of premises is obviously not appropriate in cases where mobile radioactive apparatus is used on premises not occupied by the person providing the service. Accordingly section 3 of the Act provides for the registration of users in respect of mobile equipment, such as the large gamma sources which are taken from site to site to radiograph welds.

213. The Act also requires all users, except Crown establishments and certain other specifically exempted users, to have an authorisation granted by the appropriate Minster or Ministers before disposing of radioactive waste. The application of this part of the Act to the UKAEA and nuclear site licensees has already been mentioned. Crown users are similarly controlled by administrative means. For other users the appropriate Minister is the same as for registration. These other users also require an authorisation to accumulate radioactive waste. This provision is necessary since without it waste could be produced but not discharged, eventually creating a major hazard.

214. Authorisations specify type of waste, means of disposal, conditions which must be observed, and any measurements on wastes or on the environment which may be necessary. Professional officers of the authorising Ministries inspect installations periodically to check compliance with conditions of authorisation of waste disposal. They take samples or measurements of the local environment and arrange for independent checks to be made on the activity of certain wastes.

215. If it appears that a disposal is likely to involve a public or local authority in special precautions, the Secretary of State or Ministers must consult with

that authority before the authorisation is granted. Provided that such special precautions are conditions of the authorisation, the authority can make charges for the service. The Act places a duty on local authorities to accept and deal with radioactive wastes sent to their refuse tips in accordance with an authorisation. In granting an authorisation the Secretary of State may make such conditions as he thinks fit.

216. As in the case of registration, exemption from authorisation is given in cases where an equivalent control exists or where the amount of radioactivity discharged is trivial. Such discharges must comply with the conditions of exemption given in the order, which relate to the means of disposal and the maximum quantities which can be discharged either in a given volume of non-active waste (solid) or in a given period (liquid and gaseous).

217. The Act lists in its First Schedule the legislation, other than local enactments, relating to nuisances, pollution and the discharge of wastes. The Act states that in taking action under legislation or the corresponding local enactments, no account shall be taken of any radioactivity possessed by any substance or by any part of the premises. The Act does not remove from public or local authorities any existing rights to control radioactive waste for reasons other than the radioactive content. In other words the relevant authority retains its powers in respect of, say, the chemical toxicity of radioactive waste.

218. Local authorities are kept aware of the radioactive materials held in their area and of the discharges of waste which are authorised. The Act provides that they be supplied with copies of the relevant certificates, except where national security requirements do not allow this.

219. The Act defines radioactive substances in two ways: firstly it considers natural radionuclides, and a substance is considered radioactive if it contains more than a scheduled concentration of these nuclides; secondly it defines as radioactive any substance possessing radioactivity produced by artificial bombardment with neutrons or ionising radiations. Substances contaminated by other substances are included. Thus all artificial radionuclides are included, but natural radionuclides only if above a certain concentration.

220. Radioactive waste is defined as a substance or article which, if it were not waste, would be radioactive material, or a substance or article which has been contaminated by radioactive material or waste.

221. Although local disposal of waste is the most satisfactory, there are some wastes for which this method is not appropriate. Accordingly the Act gave the Ministers power to provide other facilities. This has given rise to the National Disposal Service, which is operated on behalf of the Secretary of State by the UKAEA Atomic Energy Research Establishment (AERE) Harwell and by BNFL. Subject to authorisation suitable (intermediate activity) wastes may be

buried at the former Royal Ordnance Factory at Drigg (operated by BNFL). Wastes unsuitable for direct burial at Drigg may be dealt with at AERE, where in addition there are facilities for decontaminating working plant. Combustible wastes may be burned in a special incinerator, the ash from which, after suitable packaging, may be dumped in the sea.

Nuclear Installations Acts 1965 and 1969

222. These Acts provided the main statutory basis for the control over processing and storage of high-activity radioactive wastes arising from the nuclear power programme. The responsible Ministers, the Secretary of State for Energy and the Secretaries of State for Wales and Scotland, are advised by the NII. The NII grants licences under the Acts for the construction and operation of any installations for the manufacture, use, storage and processing of nuclear fuel, and exercises general surveillance over processing and storage of radioactive wastes at licensed sites. The UKAEA and Government Departments are not subject to the licensing requirements but maintain comparable safety standards.

223. The Nuclear Installations Act 1965 enables the United Kingdom to implement the Paris and Brussels Conventions on compensation for nuclear damage. It imposes absolute liability for damage on the operator subject to a limit of £5 million per incident, against which liability insurance is compulsory. Beyond these sums, the cost of compensating for damage is met by the Secretary of State.

Radiological Protection Act 1970

224. This Act set up the National Radiological Protection Board (NRPB) which incorporated the functions of the Radioactive Substances Advisory Committee (mentioned in paragraph 191) and the Radiological Protection Service, and took over certain radiation protection functions of the UKAEA.

Health and Safety at Work etc Act 1974

225. General protection of people at work from radioactivity and the prevention of risks to the health and safety of the general public from radioactivity which may arise from work activities lie, as does protection from other dangerous substances, with the HSE under the Health and Safety at Work etc Act 1974.

IV. ADVISORY BODIES

Nuclear Safety Advisory Committee

226. The Nuclear Safety Advisory Committee was set up by the Secretaries of State for Energy and for Scotland to provide an authoritative source of independent advice on nuclear safety issues. The Committee will probably be reconstituted to take account of the new scheme of responsibility created by the Health and Safety at Work etc Act 1974.

V. CENTRAL GOVERNMENT ADVICE

227. The main central Government circulars sent to local authorities in England and Wales on radioactivity are:

MHLG 57/59 Government action on radioactivity (WO 57/59)
      3/63 Radioactive Substances Act 1960. Explanatory memorandum for guidance of users of radioactive material (WO 3/63).

228. In Scotland, advice has been given in the following main circulars:

SDD   11/63 Radioactive Substances Act 1960
     124/75 Radioactive Substances Act 1960.

VI. INTERNATIONAL ACTION

229. International regulations and most national regulations controlling the transport of radioactive materials, including all types of radioactive wastes, conform with the model regulations developed by the UN International Atomic Energy Agency. International agreements, eg the Convention on the Prevention of Marine Pollution by Dumping of Waste and other Matter 1972 (the London Convention), also control the dumping of radioactive wastes on the sea-bed, which is a method of disposal for solid wastes of comparatively low activity.

230. Dumping in the sea is a carefully controlled exercise, usually carried out once a year under the operational control of the United Kingdom Atomic Energy Authority and in recent years jointly with certain other European countries under the auspices of the Nuclear Energy Agency, a subsidiary body of the OECD. The waste is packed into concrete lined drums which are dumped in a designated area by a specially chartered vessel. The area for the dump has been agreed internationally and is selected to clear the Continental Shelf, fishing grounds and underwater cables. The navigation of the vessel undertaking dumping is carefully observed and recorded. Within the United Kingdom the responsibility for control of disposals rests with the Fisheries Department of MAFF, who co-ordinate action with other Departments. Separate authorisations are in force for disposal of waste at sea and restrictions are placed on the type and quantity to be disposed of in this way. Transport of the waste at sea is covered by regulations under the Merchant Shipping Act (see chapter 4).

231. Within the EEC a Euratom directive on basic safety standards is in the final stages of discussion. This will ensure that the standards evolved by the ICRP are applied throughout the Community; it is being reviewed at present to bring it in line with current ICRP recommendations.

VII. MONITORING

232. Monitoring for radioactive pollution is done by a number of agencies:

(a) Much of the routine monitoring in the vicinity of a major nuclear establishment is carried out by the establishment operators.

(b) Independent checks on these measurements are carried out by the FRL on marine samples and by the Atomic Energy Branch (MAFF) using the analytical resources of the former and those of the Central Veterinary Laboratories. Independent samples procured by the Radiochemical Inspectorate are analysed by the Laboratory of the Government Chemist (Department of Industry). The same agencies are involved in the case of Wales. In Scotland the Fisheries Radiobiological Laboratories conduct independent sampling of marine specimens on behalf of their Pollution Inspectorate; the latter arrange for independent samples of other materials to be analysed by the Government Chemist and the Agricultural Research Council (ARC) Letcombe Laboratory.

(c) Measurements confirming the situation regarding weapon test fallout are currently co-ordinated by the Protection Against Ionising Radiation Committee (PIRC) of the MRC. In this field routine measurements on air and rain are made by AERE and NRPB while a continuing programme on milk is conducted by the ARC Letcombe Laboratory.

VIII. RESEARCH

233. Research and development on practical problems of radiological protection for both the public and those engaged in work is carried out by the NRPB; and the UKAEA and BNFL undertake research and development into radio-active waste management, control and disposal. The UKAEA, BNFL, the Radiochemical Centre and the Ministry of Defence Atomic Weapons Research Establishment carry out programmes of transport packaging studies which currently include comparing the fire-resisting properties of various packaging materials. Research on effects of radiation is carried out at other centres including AERE and the MRC Radiobiology Unit.

234. The FRL at Lowestoft is responsible for scientific advice on all questions arising from the disposal of radioactive waste to the sea and surface waters for the whole of the United Kingdom. It surveys all nuclear sites where dis-charges of liquid waste occur, elucidates the pathways by which radiation might thereby reach members of the public and determines the amounts of various radionuclides present in the environment. Consequently it provides the scientific advice necessary to ensure that the public is safeguarded from harmful effects of radioactive waste disposal and advises upon whatever monitoring is necessary.

235. A substantial amount of environmental research is done from the FRL. The work includes research into the behaviour of radioactivity in the marine environment and verification of the safety of a contaminated regime. The present basis for setting control measures is continually reassessed to improve the predictive capability and to ensure that the maximum standards of control are maintained. The research programme includes a continual check on monitoring and surveillance techniques used in carrying out statutory obligation of the MAFF Sea Fisheries Inspectorate.

CHAPTER 7

PESTICIDES

I. INTRODUCTION

236. Pesticides (insecticides, fungicides, herbicides, rodenticides etc) play a valuable role in the protection of growing crops, livestock and stored food. Without them farm productivity and the quality of food would fall considerably.

237. However, if pesticides are used without due care and proper regard to reasonable safety precautions, they can pose risks to users, consumers of treated produce, users of treated products and passers-by and to livestock, domestic animals, fish and beneficial insects. For a number of years successive Governments have sought through a combination of non-statutory arrangements and legislation to minimise these risks and it is fair to say that the United Kingdom's record of pesticide safety is second to none.

II. ADMINISTRATIVE ARRANGEMENTS

238. The main control of pesticides is under the non-statutory Pesticides Safety Precautions Scheme (PSPS). Under this scheme Government Departments, mainly the Ministry of Agriculture, Fisheries and Food (MAFF), the Department of Health and Social Security (DHSS) and the Health and Safety Executive (HSE)*, consider the safety of pesticides before they go into general use. The Departments and the HSE are advised by the Advisory Committee on Pesticides and other Toxic Chemicals. The scheme is described in more detail in Section V.

III. LEGISLATION

239. Various statutory measures bear either directly or indirectly on the chemical composition or use of pesticides. The main legislation includes:

   (a) Factories Act 1961
   (b) Health and Safety at Work etc Act 1974
   (c) Farm and Garden Chemicals Act 1967
   (d) Medicines Act 1968
   (e) Air Navigation Order 1974 and Rules of the Air and Air Traffic Control Regulations 1974
   (f) Rivers (Prevention of Pollution) Acts 1951 and 1961 and Control of Pollution Act 1974.

---

*In Scotland the Department of Agriculture and Fisheries for Scotland (DAFS) and the Scottish Home and Health Department (SHHD).

240. Other statutory measures which have a bearing on pesticides are the Protection of Animals Acts 1911–1927, Protection of Animals (Scotland) Act 1912, Pharmacy and Poisons Act 1933, Protection of Birds Act 1954, Food and Drugs Act 1955 as amended, Animals (Cruel Poisons) Act 1962 and Deposit of Poisonous Waste Act 1972.

Factories Act 1961

241. This Act makes statutory provision for the health and safety of workers in factories. It applies in places where pesticides are manufactured, formulated or used in industrial processes (eg moth-proofing).

Health and Safety at Work etc Act 1974

242. This Act imposes general obligations on:
  (a) employers to ensure so far as reasonably practicable the health, safety and welfare at work of their employees;
  (b) the self-employed and employees to take reasonable care of their own health and safety at work;
  (c) employers, the self-employed and employees not to put at risk, by their work activities, the health and safety of others;
  (d) manufacturers, importers and suppliers of substances for use at work to ensure, so far as reasonably practicable, that the substances are safe and without risks to health when properly used.

243. Under the Act Ministers are empowered to make Regulations regulating or prohibiting inter alia the manufacture, supply, keeping or use of any substance.

Health and Safety (Agriculture) (Poisonous Substances) Regulations 1975

244. These Regulations, made under the Health and Safety at Work etc Act, impose obligations on employers, employees and the self-employed. They are designed to protect operators from poisoning by the more toxic pesticides by ensuring amongst other things that they are supplied with, and use, adequate protective clothing when working with these compounds in agriculture (including work in enclosed buildings such as greenhouses and livestock houses).

245. The Regulations name 60 active ingredients of pesticides, group them into four classes and describe 26 operations for which operators must wear specified protective clothing according to the class of active ingredient used and the type of operation. The Regulations were founded on advice given by the Advisory Committee on Pesticides and Other Toxic Chemicals.

Farm and Garden Chemicals Act 1967

246. This Act empowers the Minister of Agriculture, Fisheries and Food and the Secretary of State for Scotland jointly to make regulations governing the

labelling of pesticides intended for sale for plant protection purposes in agriculture or gardening. Regulations may require:

(a) the names of active ingredients to appear on the label

(b) the label to bear a prescribed mark, symbol or colour to indicate the extent of risk which the hazard constitutes to human beings or to other forms of life and to bear prescribed words of explanation or warning.

247. The Farm and Garden Chemicals Regulations 1971, which came into effect on 1 May 1973, require farm and garden pesticides to be labelled clearly and conspicuously with the names of any scheduled active ingredients they contain.

Medicines Act 1968

248. The small amounts of pesticides used in medical and veterinary products are subject to statutory control under the Medicines Act 1968. The Act provides for the control of medicinal products and certain other substances and articles through a system of product licences and certificates and the licensing of firms and persons engaged in the manufacture of or wholesale dealing in the products. Under the Act it is unlawful to manufacture, sell, supply or import products covered by the Act except in accordance with the appropriate licences or exemptions. Advertising and labelling of these products can also be controlled under the Act. Licences for human medicines are issued by DHSS and those for veterinary medicines by MAFF. The licensing authorities are advised with respect to the safety, quality or efficacy of the products by the Committee on Safety of Medicines and the Veterinary Products Committee. Safety is in practice interpreted very widely to include the safety of the environment ie wildlife, water courses etc.

Air Navigation Order 1974 and Rules of the Air and Air Traffic Control Regulations 1974

249. Under this civil aviation legislation aerial spraying of pesticides is controlled by the Civil Aviation Authority and detailed arrangements are laid down in a document entitled "The Aerial Application Permission—Requirements and Information". These include the provision that only pesticides which appear in a "permitted list", all of which have been specifically cleared for this purpose under the Pesticides Safety Precautions Scheme (see paragraph 253), may be sprayed from the air.

Rivers (Prevention of Pollution) Acts 1951 and 1961 and Control of Pollution Act 1974

250. The Rivers (Prevention of Pollution) Acts 1951 and 1961 (see Chapter 6) make it an offence to cause poisonous, noxious, or polluting matter to enter a stream; this indirectly can control the levels of pesticides in effluents accepted into the public sewer and in discharges to rivers etc. Discharges to estuaries

or to coastal waters will be controlled in a similar way in future by Part II of the Control of Pollution Act 1974.

251. The Oslo and London Dumping Conventions not only control the dumping of toxic wastes (including pesticides) at sea but also require that the best practicable means be used to prevent the pollution of the sea by persistent pesticides. There is also United Kingdom legislation which relates specifically to the protection of waters containing fish from poisonous matter or trade effluents. Water authorities are empowered to make byelaws regulating the deposit or discharge, in any waters containing fish, of any liquid or solid matter detrimental to salmon, trout or freshwater fish, or the spawn or food of fish.

IV. ADVISORY BODIES

Advisory Committee on Pesticides and Other Toxic Chemicals

252. This Committee, which is appointed by the Secretary of State for Education and Science and serviced by MAFF, is the principal source of advice to Government on pesticides. Its membership includes both official and independent members under an independent Chairman. It is supported by a Scientific Sub-Committee which includes experts in toxicology, chemistry, pharmacology, plant pathology, entomology, carcinogenic hazards, veterinary science and wildlife hazards, and by specialist panels on eg residues in food (see paragraph 264) and wildlife hazards.

V. NON-STATUTORY CONTROLS

Pesticides Safety Precautions Scheme (PSPS)

253. Through the operation of PSPS the Government exercises a very close supervision over the introduction of pesticides

(i)   for use in the United Kingdom in or near water, in agriculture (including animal husbandry), horticulture, forestry, the home (including home gardens) and food storage and as wood preservatives

(ii) for all uses by central and local Government, public authorities and servicing companies

(iii) for closely related uses, eg herbicides used in or around industrial premises.

The Scheme is non-statutory but is a formally negotiated agreement between the Government and the pesticides industry under which manufacturers have undertaken to notify MAFF or HSE before marketing any new pesticide or suggesting a new use of an existing one.

254. The manufacturer notifying a pesticide must provide sufficient data to enable MAFF and DHSS (DAFS and SHHD in Scotland) and HSE to decide whether the pesticide can be used without harming human beings (including users and consumers of treated crops of food), livestock or domestic animals and with minimum harm to wild life, provided reasonable safety precautions

are taken. The data required may include information on the physical, chemical and biological properties of the pesticide concerned, eg its persistence in crops and in the soil, the products into which it may break down in the plant and its mode of action; on experimental work on its toxicity to mammals and, where available, to man; and on its likely effects on wild life, including birds, fish and bees. In addition the proposed use and method of application of the product must be given, together with information about possible risks arising from its use. Methods of analysis, medical data and sometimes any particulars of its use in other countries are also required.

255. Before reaching a decision on a notification Departments may seek the advice of the Scientific Subcommittee of the Advisory Committee on Pesticides and Other Toxic Chemicals. In the light of scientific evidence before it (from the manufacturer and from other sources) and provided it believes it can safely do so, the Subcommittee drafts recommendations for the safe use of the pesticide with special regard to the protection of users, consumers of treated crops or foodstuffs, and wild life. If the Subcommittee is not satisfied with the data it can ask the manufacturers to carry out further experimental work. The draft recommendations normally go to the Advisory Committee on Pesticides and Other Toxic Chemicals which considers them from other than the purely scientific point of view. The Advisory Committee's recommendations then go forward to the appropriate Government Departments who may accept or modify the proposals before they are sent to the manufacturer for comment and ultimately issued as official recommendations sheets.

257. The recommendations sheets cover advice on the protection of users, of consumers of treated crops and foodstuffs, of third parties, and of livestock, domestic animals and wildlife. They have a wide circulation including public health and local authorities, merchants' and manufacturers' associations (and through them their members), the official advisory services and numerous trade journals. Manufacturers are required under the scheme to include the warnings and precautions and the name of the active ingredients on their product labels. In this way users of pesticides receive official warnings and advice on the safe use of pesticides from product labels, from their trade journals or through members of the official advisory services.

257. The PSPS also includes machinery to ensure that the use of any pesticide may be reviewed by the Advisory Committee in the event of any new scientific evidence coming to light about risks which could not have been envisaged at the time the pesticide was originally cleared. Pesticides used in other industrial or manufacturing processes (ie other than food storage and wood preservation) are being brought into the scheme after consultation with interested parties.

Agricultural Chemicals Approval Scheme

258. This is a voluntary scheme under which proprietary brands of crop protection chemicals (insecticides, fungicides and herbicides etc) given clearance under the PSPS can be submitted for official "approval" of their biological

efficiency. The purpose of the scheme is to enable users to select, and advisers to recommend, efficient and appropriate crop protection chemicals for use against particular pests and to discourage the use of unsatisfactory products. The scheme covers only those chemicals used for the control of plant pests and diseases, for the destruction of weeds, for growth regulation and certain other crop protection purposes and for the control of insect and mite pests of farm stored grain. It does not cover rodenticides, pesticides used for food storage generally or veterinary or domestic (other than home garden) products.

259. The scheme is operated by the Agricultural Chemicals Approval Organisation on behalf of MAFF and DAFS. Approval is granted by the Organisation for specific uses only when it is satisfied that the product fulfils the claims made on the label. Labels are subject to constant review. Approved products bear the "A" symbol on the label; a list of approved products for farmers and growers is issued annually.

VI. INTERNATIONAL ACTION

260. The programmes of a number of international organisations are concerned with the control of pesticides. The terms of reference of the Council of Europe Public Health Committee's Sub-Committee on Poisonous Substances in Agriculture include the study of the risk to human health arising from the use of pesticides in agriculture and food storage and the study of ways and means of preventing pesticide residues in food as far as possible. In addition the Committee makes recommendations designed to ensure the safe use of pesticides with the hope that member states will incorporate these recommendations into the practices followed in their respective countries.

261. The Codex Committee on Pesticide Residues, a subsidiary body of the Codex Alimentarius Commission of the Food and Agriculture and World Health Organisations of the United Nations, is responsible for proposing international tolerances for pesticide residues in specific foods. Its aims are to protect the health of the consumer, to ensure fair practices in the food trade and to facilitate international trade.

262. The EEC is also active in the field of pesticides. A draft directive on pesticide residues in fruit and vegetables is under discussion and it is intended that other commodities will be the subject of further directives. In addition a draft directive has been prepared which would require member states to harmonise national legislative and/or administrative arrangements for the classification, packaging and labelling of pesticide preparations.

263. The EEC Commission has been working on proposals for a draft directive on securing the acceptance throughout the EEC of plant protection products whereby manufacturers could, if they so wished, apply to any member country to have a product cleared for safety and efficacy under the terms of the directive. Formulations which had been cleared under this scheme would (with certain safeguards) be allowed free circulation throughout the Community. This

Community scheme would operate in parallel with member countries' own national pesticide registration schemes.

VII. MONITORING

264. The Scientific Subcommittee of the Advisory Committee on Pesticides and other Toxic Chemicals has a Panel for the Collection of Residue Data which is responsible for organising the monitoring of foodstuffs for pesticide residue. This Panel was set up in 1969 (in succession to an earlier body)

  (i) to review information from any source on levels of pesticides and derivatives of pesticides in human food;

  (ii) to arrange selective or comprehensive surveys of pesticide residue levels in food; and

  (iii) to arrange surveys of pesticide residue levels in the environment where this is considered to be relevant to residue levels in food.

265. Most of the analytical work involved in the Government monitoring programmes for individual foodstuffs is divided among six participating laboratories: the Laboratory of the Government Chemist (Department of Industry), MAFF's Plant Pathology Laboratory at Harpenden, Pest Infestation Control Laboratory at Slough and Fisheries Laboratory at Lowestoft and the DAFS Agricultural Scientific Services Laboratory at Edinburgh and Freshwater Fisheries Laboratory at Pitlochry. The Association of Public Analysts, together with the local authorities associations have carried out three Joint Surveys of Pesticide Residues in Foodstuffs sold in England and Wales.

266. Units based at MAFF's Plant Pathology Laboratory and the DAFS Agricultural Scientific Services Laboratory collect usage data on agricultural pesticides and a unit based at MAFF's Pest Infestation Control Laboratory collects data on usage in food storage in collaboration with DAFS.

267. Pesticide residues in wildlife are monitored by the MAFF Pest Infestation Control Laboratory and the DAFS Agricultural Scientific Services Laboratory and also in a joint Nature Conservancy Council (NCC)/Natural Environmental Research Council (NERC) study. In addition, the Organisation for Economic Co-operation and Development has established an international programme of monitoring to determine trends in pesticide residues in animals in different countries. Information on pesticide pollution is also collected in the course of other monitoring, eg analysis by water authorities of river samples.

VIII. RESEARCH

268. Research on pesticides is carried out at the last five of the laboratories mentioned in paragraph 265, at the Monks Wood Experimental Station (part of the Institute of Terrestrial Ecology), the Agricultural Research Council's (ARC's) Experimental Station at Rothamsted and many other organisations. The ARC's Weed Research Organisation carries out research on herbicides.

CHAPTER 8

NOISE

I. INTRODUCTION

269. In the modern world there is a continuing demand for the abundant goods and services which flow from today's technology. We take for granted the operation of powerful transport systems which apart from supplying our daily needs also allow us to travel easily and quickly to anywhere in the world for business or pleasure. These advances in the scale and power of productive processes have, however, greatly increased the level of background noise to which we are all subject, particularly those of us who live and work in the crowded urban areas. It is no wonder that the last twenty years have seen an ever-growing public concern about noise, the wrong sound in the wrong place, which has come to be acknowledged as pollution in yet another guise.

270. When the statutory nuisance provisions of the Public Health (Scotland) Act 1897 and the Public Health Act 1936 were framed noise was not regarded as of sufficient concern to merit inclusion, and it was not until the Noise Abatement Act 1960 was passed that local authorities could take action against noise as well as smells, dust and dirt. The law was strengthened by the Public Health (Recurring Nuisances) Acts 1969 under which local authorities in England and Wales could prohibit the recurrence of a nuisance, including noise. By exercising their powers under this legislation local authorities were able to make life more tolerable. In many cases they were able to achieve this through informal action and the co-operation of those responsible.

271. This legislation was however very restrictive. Procedures tended to be complicated and to work in favour of the noise maker and penalties were small. Moreover it was still difficult for local authorities to tackle some of the most serious noise problems, particularly since they could only act after the noise had been made. More important, they could not take positive action to secure a real and lasting reduction in environmental noise levels. The Noise Advisory Council (see paragraphs 291 and 292 below) reviewed the existing legal position in 1970 and its recommendations, contained in its report "Neighbourhood Noise", formed the basis of the noise provisions in the Control of Pollution Act 1974. This improves and strengthens local authorities' existing powers, introduces special controls over construction and demolition sites and gives local authorities power to set up noise abatement zones. These provisions are discussed in detail in paragraphs 287–290 below.

272. All this legislation was, and is, directed at noise in the environment generally (known collectively as neighbourhood noise) and it has always been left to specific legislation to deal with noise from three other main sources—

70

road traffic, air traffic and industrial premises. Much of this legislation is comparatively recent.

273. Road traffic disturbs more people than all other forms of noise nuisance combined. The most disturbing features are its general level and its variability with time—variations at different times of day (due to changes in traffic volumes and the type of vehicle passing) and short term variations as individual vehicles pass. Whereas traffic noise has been steadily increasing over the last few decades, serious disturbance from civil aircraft noise suddenly became widespread with the introduction of the jet engine in the late 1950s and over the last few years both densely populated areas and quieter rural areas have become affected. Noise within industrial premises involves the exposure of those engaged in many occupations to high levels of noise which may interfere with communication or cause damage to hearing.

II. ADMINISTRATIVE ARRANGEMENTS

274. Responsibility for the control of noise is divided between several Ministers. The Secretaries of State for Transport and the Environment are responsible for legislation concerned with traffic, vehicle and neighbourhood noise and they are advised by two main research establishments, the Transport and Road Research Laboratory (TRRL) and the Building Research Establishment (BRE), on the technical issues involved. Road vehicle noise legislation for vehicles in use is enforced by the police; neighbourhood noise is controlled by local authorities. The Secretary of State for Trade has general responsibility for aircraft noise in the United Kingdom, and detailed responsibility for noise abatement for designated airports (see paragraph 281). Controls are administered by the airport management. The Secretary of State for Employment is mainly responsible for legislation on noise within workplaces, which is administered and enforced by the Health and Safety Executive (HSE) (see paragraph 284). The Secretaries of State for Wales and for Scotland are responsible for traffic and neighbourhood noise controls within Wales and Scotland.

III. LEGISLATION

275. The principal statutes governing noise are as follows:
   (a) Road Traffic Acts 1972 and 1974
   (b) Land Compensation Act 1973 and Land Compensation (Scotland) Act 1973
   (c) Civil Aviation Acts 1949, 1968 and 1971
   (d) Airports Authority (Consolidation) Act 1975
   (e) Air Navigation (Noise Certification) Order 1970
   (f) Health and Safety at Work etc Act 1974
   (g) Noise Abatement Act 1960
   (h) Public Health (Recurring Nuisances) Act 1969
   (i) Control of Pollution Act 1974.

Road Traffic Acts 1972 and 1974

276. The earliest regulations designed to reduce the amount of noise emitted by road vehicles were of a general nature relating to the fitting of a silencer and these are now contained in the Motor Vehicles (Construction and Use) Regulations 1973. The regulations require this silencer to be maintained in efficient working order and also prohibit excessive noise due either to negligence of the driver or to poor maintenance. In 1970 maximum noise limits were introduced for all types of vehicle and these also are specfied in the regulations. Enforcement in service is a police responsibility. As well as maximum permitted noise levels for vehicles in use, test procedures are prescribed in the regulations but owing to the many other duties falling on the police, very few such checks are carried out. The inclusion of a check on the condition of the exhaust system and silencers in the "MOT test" for cars has been agreed and should come into effect during 1976.

277. As regards the enforcement of construction standards, the Road Traffic Act 1974 provides for the operation of a compulsory national type approval scheme, and the first part of this will be introduced in 1977 (starting with passenger cars). Under this scheme, before marketing a new type of vehicle, the manufacturer will have to produce a sample production vehicle for testing by the Department of Transport. The vehicle will have to comply with all relevant safety and environmental standards and the manufacturer will have to demonstrate that he has adequate quality assurance procedures. He will be required to certify that every vehicle sold conforms to an approved type and random checks will be made to ensure that this is so. Also it will be an offence to sell or fit an important replacement part (eg a silencer) if it is not of an approved type.

278. Much has been done and much more will be achieved in the future to reduce rates of vehicle noise at source, but undeniably many people will continue to be disturbed and annoyed by it. Steps can however be taken to protect people through traffic management schemes and special routeings designed to take, where practicable, the traffic away from as many people as possible. Under the Road Traffic Regulation Act 1967 local highway authorities and the Secretary of State for Transport can make traffic regulation orders prohibiting or restricting the use of a road by some or all traffic. These powers have been reinforced by the Heavy Commercial Vehicles (Controls and Regulations) Act 1973 which gives local authorities powers to make traffic regulation orders prohibiting or restricting the use of heavy commercial vehicles on specified routes. They may also specify the routes that such vehicles must follow. Consideration is currently being given by the Department of Transport to the setting up of a national network of routes for the heaviest of lorries.

Land Compensation Act 1973

279. The Noise Insulation Regulations 1973 made under the Land Compensation Act 1973, and the Noise Insulation (Scotland) Regulations 1975 made

under the Land Compensation (Scotland) Act 1973, allow the insulation of dwellings against traffic noise from new or improved roads with the benefit of a grant from the highway authority. The same Act also allows the highway authority to acquire land for the erection of remedial works, such as earth embankments and acoustic barriers, to mitigate any adverse effects from the use of the road.

Civil Aviation Acts 1949, 1968 and 1971 and Airport Authority (Consolidation) Act 1975

280. The Civil Aviation Act 1949 (as amended by the Civil Aviation Act 1968) provides for the prohibition of any aircraft landing or taking off in the United Kingdom unless it has a noise certificate and is complying with the certificate's requirements. The scheme is based on international agreements drawn up within the International Civil Aviation Organisation. The Civil Aviation Authority (CAA) is responsible for the day to day administration but is required to consult the Secretary of State for Trade about the classes of aircraft to which the scheme applies.

281. The Secretary of State for Trade may designate an airport for noise abatement under section 29 of the Civil Aviation Act 1971. To date Heathrow, Gatwick, Stansted and Prestwick Airports have been designated. At these airports the noise abatement measures prescribed by the Secretary of State include minimum noise routes, rates of climb, flying heights, general instructions about avoiding built-up areas, and restrictions on night movements of jets at Heathrow and Gatwick. A number of airports are owned and managed by local authorities or private owners, who are responsible for noise control at their airports. At some of those owned by the local authorities, noise abatement measures including minimum noise routes (and at Manchester and Luton restrictions on night movements of jets) have been introduced under local act and general management powers. Noise abatement measures at designated airports are agreed initially between airport management, the Department of Trade (DT) and the CAA and when introduced are administered by the airport management. At non-designated airports the measures are agreed between the airport management and the CAA and are then administered by the former.

282. In spite of noise control and abatement measures and the introduction of quieter aircraft people living in the vicinity of airports continue to be seriously disturbed. Section 29(a) of the Civil Aviation Act 1971, incorporated in Schedule 5 of the Airports Authority (Consolidation) Act 1975, gives the Secretary of State for Trade powers to make schemes for designated airports requiring the management to make grants towards the cost of insulating buildings against aircraft noise. At non-designated airports similar schemes may be introduced by the airport management under local act powers.

Air Navigation (Noise Certification) Order 1970

283. Many new types of subsonic aircraft, such as the Lockheed TriStar, are

substantially quieter than their predecessors. In the United Kingdom new types whose certificates of airworthiness were issued on or after 1 January 1976 have to meet the requirements of the Air Navigation (Noise Certification) Order 1970, the provisions of which are based upon agreements with the International Civil Aviation Organisation. These requirements have the effect that aircraft of new design should be only half as noisy as pre-1969 designs of similar weight already in service. But of course older aircraft continue to be flown in substantial numbers, as the average life of a commercial aircraft is 15 years. Even so, some reductions in noise have been made on a number of types of such aircraft.

Health and Safety at Work etc Act 1974

284. Under the Health and Safety at Work etc Act 1974 it is the general duty of employers to ensure as far as is reasonably practicable the health, safety and welfare of their employees. The Health and Safety Commission established under the Act has overall responsibility for occupational safety and health. The legislation is administered and enforced by the Health and Safety Executive (HSE), which incorporates the former Factory Inspectorate.

Noise Abatement Act 1960

285. Neighbourhood noise is a wide term embracing a variety of stationary sources of noise which cause disturbance and annoyance. It can include noise from factories, sports stadia, places of entertainment, construction and demolition sites, roadworks, and community noise arising from lack of consideration, for example from amplifiers, noisy parties, and the slamming of car doors.

286. The principal control over neighbourhood noise comes from the 1960 Noise Abatement Act, under which local authorities have power to deal with noise nuisance. The Act is primarily designed to deal with noise from fixed sources, eg industrial and domestic premises. In England and Wales the Act has now been replaced by the provisions of the Control of Pollution Act 1974.

Control of Pollution Act 1974

287. Part III of the Control of Pollution Act 1974 was implemented in England and Wales on 1 January 1976. (Implementation in Scotland is still under consideration.) It strengthens the similar provisions in the Noise Abatement Act 1960 to control noise nuisance and should make enforcement more effective, because a person on whom a noise abatement notice has been served will be expected to comply with the notice if he does not appeal within 21 days to the Magistrates' Court (or, when the Act is implemented in Scotland, Sheriff Court). Under the Noise Abatement Act the noise nuisance could continue until the local authority had succeeded in getting the notice enforced by the courts. Maximum penalties for non-compliance have been substantially increased and now stand at £200 for the first offence and £400 for the second or subsequent offence. Statutory undertakers who were excluded from the terms of the 1960 Act have been included within the scope of these provisions. A further improve-

ment is that occupiers of the premises affected by the noise may complain individually to a Magistrates' Court (or, in Scotland, Sheriff Court) instead of having to get the support of at least two other occupiers of premises similarly affected. Such complaints may be made independently of any action taken by a local authority. There is also provision to allow the Secretary of State to issue or approve codes of practice offering guidance to operators and local authorities on the best use of such potentially troublesome devices as burglar alarms, ice-cream van-chimes and acoustic bird-scarers. This should greatly assist local authorities in defining what constitutes a nuisance.

288. The Act contains a new provision related to noise from construction sites. Under section 60 the local authority may serve a notice imposing requirements as to the way in which the works are to be carried out and these may cover the plant or the machinery to be used, the hours of working and the permissible levels of noise from the site. Alternatively, under section 61, the persons responsible for carrying out the works may ask the local authority to specify its noise requirements before these works actually begin. In both cases appeals against local authority requirements are provided for. A code of practice has been drawn up by the British Standards Institution setting out guidelines for the control of noise on construction and demolition sites.

289. Another new provision of the Act is the power to establish noise abatement zones. This is a completely new concept and is mainly directed against noises from fixed sources such as factories and commercial premises. Its aim is to secure a positive reduction in noise levels. A local authority may declare a single site or an area to be a noise abatement zone and may then measure existing noise levels emanating from these classified premises. These levels will be entered into a noise level register and it will be an offence to exceed them without the permission of the local authority. More importantly the authority may require these measured levels to be reduced, though it must have regard, amongst other things, to the best practicable means available in order to meet any such requirements. This means taking into account local conditions and circumstances, the limitations of current technical knowledge and the financial implications. In other words a local authority cannot make unreasonable requirements.

290. The Act deliberately avoids laying down any kind of environmental standards to be applied nationally and it gives no indication of what local authorities might regard as acceptable. Noise has always been regarded as a local phenomenon and one which should be dealt with locally. Standards which might be too stringent in one situation might not be sufficiently stringent in another.

IV. ADVISORY BODIES

291. The Noise Advisory Council was set up in 1970 to advise the Secretary of

State for the Environment, who is also its Chairman. It has the following terms of reference:

"to keep under review progress made generally in preventing and abating the generation of noise; to make recommendations to Ministers with responsibility in this field; and to advise on such matters as they may refer to the Council".

292. The Council consists of 22 members, one of whom is appointed from Wales and one from Scotland in consultation with the respective Secretaries of State. It operates through a series of working groups which provide the basis for the Council's continuing work. The Council has published a number of reports which are listed in the bibliography.

V. CENTRAL GOVERNMENT ADVICE

293. The main Government circulars on noise sent to local authorities are:

MHLG 22/67 Noise—industrial noise (WO 18/67, SDD 20/67)
MHLG 36/69 Noise—industrial noise (WO 32/69, SDD 28/69)
DOE 10/73 Planning and noise (WO 16/73, SDD 23/73)
2/76 Control of Pollution Act 1974. Implementation of Part 3— Noise (WO 3/76).

294. Abatement of existing nuisances can relieve situations already in being, but the task of positive planning is to ensure that people are not subjected to adverse noise in the developments of the future. The 1973 circular on planning and noise states that there should be a strong presumption against permitting residential developments when road noise levels measured outside dwellings over the 18 hours from 6 am to midnight exceeds 70 dB (A) for 10% of the time (L10 (18 hour)). A design bulletin ("New Housing and Road Traffic Noise") gives further guidance on the protection of residential property and advises that the building specification should be such that no dwelling has an internal L10 with windows closed greater than 50 dB (A). This is seen as a minimum standard and a "good" standard is regarded as 40 dB (A).

295. For aircraft noise local authorities are given detailed guidance according to the type of development proposed and the Noise and Number Index (NNI) contour within which it will come. The NNI is based on the average peak noise at ground level and the number of flights over a particular site.

296. Planning authorities are urged to avoid creating situations in which new commercial and industrial development might inflict noise annoyance in existing developments. The circulars advise that where at all possible ambient noise levels should not be increased. In urban areas where existing levels are already likely to be high the circulars suggest that the ambient level affecting existing residential and other noise sensitive development should not exceed a corrected noise level of 75 dB (A) by day or 65 dB (A) by night.

297. Advice on the hazards to hearing from industrial noise and on measures to reduce noise levels and protect employed persons is contained in the "Code of practice for reducing the exposure of employed persons to noise" published by the Department of Employment (DE) in 1972. Further advisory documents may also be published from time to time by HSE. The Health and Safety Commission have decided that new regulations on occupational noise are needed. HSE is consulting interested parties on the framing of such regulations; it is expected that they will follow broadly the lines of the 1972 Code of Practice.

VI. INTERNATIONAL ACTION

298. In the European Economic Community a directive sets common standards for vehicle noise levels which are applicable to all member states. Following a United Kingdom initiative a proposal is under discussion to make these standards more stringent. The long term aim is to introduce by the early 1980's noise limits which will represent a halving of the apparent loudness of heavy vehicles compared with 1975 levels.

299. As part of its long term programme, under Article 100 of the Treaty of Rome, to eliminate the technical barriers to trade between member countries, the European Commission have proposed directives relating to permissible noise levels for construction equipment and other machinery. The effect of these and future directives will be to ensure that member states cannot prevent the import from other member countries of machinery which meets the agreed standards. They may also impose the further requirement that all new machines for use within the EEC must comply with the relevant standards. Furthermore, the Commission have in hand the setting of general criteria for acceptable levels of noise in the Community as a whole.

300. Aircraft noise is also subject to international agreements through the International Civil Aviation Organisation (see paragraph 280).

VII. MONITORING

301. Measurements of noise levels are made by the various bodies concerned with its control, eg by local authority Environmental Health Officers for neighbourhood noise. With occupational noise, employers are recommended to carry out monitoring to ensure that levels remain consistently within the limits that are desirable. There is a comprehensive monitoring system around Heathrow Airport maintained by the British Airports Authority to help to ensure that civil transport aircraft do not violate the statutory limits. The efficacy of this monitoring is kept under constant review.

VIII. RESEARCH

302. Investigation of vehicle noise problems and their effect on human health and behaviour is continuing, and TRRL are carrying out research on the measurement of noise levels and associated traffic densities in urban situations

and from this it is hoped to evolve a mathematical model to predict noise levels from given traffic flows. Studies are also being carried out on the relationship between vehicle noise levels and human reaction. Of particular importance is the joint project being carried out by the Government, the Motor Industry Research Association, Southampton University Institute of Sound and Vibration Research, TRRL, and manufacturing industry to develop prototypes of heavy vehicles which will give a satisfactory performance at an acceptable cost together with a much lower noise level. The aim in fact is to cut by half the existing noise levels of such vehicles. Research into the acoustic problems of buildings and noise from industrial premises is carried out at BRE.

303. Research is being done in the aircraft and aero-engine industries using company resources and under contract to the Government, which also does research at its own establishments such as the National Gas Turbine Establishment, the National Physical Laboratory and the Royal Aircraft Establishment. The Medical Research Council and CAA are also involved. The main areas of work are:

—the quietening of aircraft, both as regards the engine and the airframe;
—effectiveness of noise abatement measures;
—subjective response to aircraft noise and its effect on health and hearing;
—the effects of operational techniques in the reduction of noise on takeoff, landing and in flight.

304. Information on research on industrial noise and related subjects is contained in the DE's industrial health and safety register of research, which can be obtained free of charge from that Department.

CHAPTER 9

INTERNATIONAL ASPECTS

I. INTRODUCTION

305. Pollution control measures may be taken not only independently by individual countries but also through international or bilateral agreements. The most important organisations in this field with which the United Kingdom is involved are the European Economic Communities (EEC), the Organisation for Economic Co-operation and Development (OECD), the United Nations Environment Programme (UNEP), NATO's Committee on the Challenges of Modern Society (CCMS) and the United Nations Economic Commission for Europe (ECE).

II. EUROPEAN COMMUNITIES

306. At the Paris summit meeting in October 1972 it was agreed that there should be a Community environment programme and the content of the first such programme was agreed at a Council of Ministers meeting in July 1973. The text of the programme was subsequently published in the Official Journal of the European Communities, vol. 16 No. C112 of 20 December 1973.

307. The basic objective of the environment programme is seen as improving the setting and quality of life and people's surroundings and living conditions. The programme falls into two main parts. The first part outlines proposals for the reduction of pollution and nuisances. It includes studies on the degree of risk to human health and the functioning of the environment posed by different substances, the development of environmental quality objectives and the formulation of standards for specific products as a means of achieving environmental quality. It also includes proposals for research projects, economic studies and the development of environmental information systems. The second main part is concerned with proposals for the improvement of the environment. It is more tentatively drawn and includes references to work on the problems of urbanisation and the natural and working environments. A second programme is under discussion.

308. The Commission of the European Communities has the responsibility for drawing up proposals under the programme and these are considered by the representatives of member states in the Council. They are also considered by the European Parliament and the Economic and Social Committee. Once adopted, EEC legislation is legally binding in member states.

309. Three Councils of Environment Ministers have been held to date, in November 1974 and in October and December 1975. A number of proposals have been adopted. These include the acceptance by the Community of the

"Polluter Pays" principle, a resolution on energy and the environment, and decisions enabling the Community to sign the Paris Convention on the prevention of marine pollution from land based sources and to set up a common inventory of sources of information on the environment. Proposals for directives adopted so far cover such subjects as the quality of surface water intended for drinking, the disposal of waste oils, the sulphur content of gas oils and the quality of bathing water.

310. A number of draft directives are currently under discussion in the Council, and the Commission is developing others for future consideration. Draft directives related to specific sectors of the environment are mentioned in the earlier chapters, but there are also some that relate to chemicals of general environmental significance, eg polychloride biphenyls (PCBs) and vinyl chloride monomers (VCMs). Proposals for directives and other instruments are published in the Official Journal, as are the final versions on adoption; copies are obtainable from HMSO.

311. The European Chemical Data and Information Network (ECDIN) is currently a pilot-project to test a design for a data bank on environmentally significant chemicals to meet the Community needs. The objective is to provide a rapid response system to meet the information needs of those responsible for decision-taking on environmental matters at both government and industrial levels. The ECDIN system should be compatible with the UNEP International Register of Potentially Toxic Chemicals (IRPTC) to facilitate two-way exchanges and the United Kingdom contributions would be channelled through our proposed national Data Network on Environmentally Significant Chemicals (DESCNET).

III. ORGANISATION FOR ECONOMIC CO-OPERATION AND DEVELOPMENT

312. The OECD brings together the major western industrialised countries, thus providing a forum for discussion of common problems and co-ordination of policies. Its Environment Committee was set up in 1970 reflecting the requirement to make economic growth qualitative as well as quantitative. Its first five year mandate was renewed in 1975 and remains very much the same in substance. It conducts investigations and proposes solutions to common environmental problems, while taking into account economic and other factors. The Committee does not get involved directly in research which is better carried out in specialised establishments, but draws heavily on the experience and expertise of such places.

313. The Committee has carried out useful work on such subjects as the "Polluter Pays" principle and its implementation; long range transport of air pollutants; eutrophication; detergents; the environmental impact of the motor vehicle, and control of certain chemicals. Work is continuing in most of these areas as well as on other subjects amongst which are transfrontier pollution,

environmental impacts of energy production and traffic restraint. Many of the Committee's studies are published and are available to the general public.

IV. UNITED NATIONS ENVIRONMENT PROGRAMME (UNEP)

314. UNEP was set up as a result of the Stockholm Conference on the Human Environment held in June 1972. A comparatively small secretariat based in Nairobi, Kenya, is responsible to a 58-nation Governing Council on which the United Kingdom has been represented since the Council was formed. The programme is supported by a voluntary Environment Fund and the Department of the Environment (DOE) is responsible for the United Kingdom contribution. This fund is intended to act as a catalyst and to back UNEP's unique role within the UN system as a co-ordinating rather than an executive agency. DOE is the focal point for co-ordinating United Kingdom responses to UNEP.

315. At the fourth session of the Governing Council which took place in Nairobi during April 1976, it was confirmed that the following should be regarded as priority subject areas:

Human Settlements and Human Health;
Ecosystems;
Environment and Development;
Oceans;
Energy;
Natural Disasters.

316. In its support of UNEP the United Kingdom is especially concerned with two UNEP initiatives. The first of these, Earthwatch, has two main components, the International Referral Service for Sources of Environmental Information (IRS) and the Global Environmental Monitoring System (GEMS). The United Kingdom has been involved in much of the basic design work of the IRS and is establishing the United Kingdom national counterpart (NRS) to this international service. The United Kingdom is also working towards a comprehensive flexible and unified environmental monitoring system which reflects the longer term aim of the UNEP Global Environmental Monitoring System and will provide consolidated national input to GEMS.

317. The second UNEP programme with which the United Kingdom is particularly concerned is IRPTC. This should provide essential data on environmentally significant chemicals to meet one of the requirements for the operation of the early warning capability being developed within the relevant sections of UNEP. It is hoped to facilitate data exchange on a global basis relating to such chemicals including policies, regulatory measures, criteria and standards by designing a network to access existing data collections. Our direct national input should be channelled through DESCNET to IRPTC but this would not detract from our commitments to EEC on ECDIN. Within the other priority subject areas, the United Kingdom's main interests lie in Human Health and Ecosystems.

V. COMMITTEE ON THE CHALLENGES OF MODERN SOCIETY (CCMS)

318. In 1969 the North Atlantic Treaty Organisation (NATO) established as a subsidiary body the CCMS for the purpose of undertaking international studies of specific problems of the human environment. The objective was to stimulate the exchange of experience and technical knowledge and to put the findings into practice. Studies are normally carried out under the leadership of one or more member countries. Studies have been initiated over a wide range of environmental problems including the disposal of hazardous wastes; coastal water pollution; inland water pollution; air pollution; and advanced waste water treatment.

319. Participation in a study is undertaken on a voluntary basis, and as a general rule member countries take part only where they can usefully contribute or obtain tangible benefits. The United Kingdom has taken the lead in some studies including ones on advanced waste water treatment and landfill research (under the disposal of hazardous wastes study).

VI. ECONOMIC COMMISSION FOR EUROPE

320. In 1971 the United Nations Economic Commission for Europe, which covers the whole of Europe and North America, including the USSR and the countries which are members of the Council for Mutual Economic Assistance, set up as one of its principal subsidiary bodies the Senior Advisers to ECE Governments on Environmental Problems. At present the Senior Advisers are giving priority to projects on environmental impact assessment, integration of environmental policies into socio-economic planning development, non-waste technology, air pollution, noise, energy and transportation. They are also working on information systems and exchange, land-use planning, solid and toxic wastes and biodegradable substances. These priorities have been revised to take account, among other things, of the Final Act of the Conference on Security and Co-operation in Europe. A number of other studies to which the Senior Advisers contribute are being run within the ECE. The Senior Advisers also work in close liaison with the ECE Committee on Water Problems and with UNEP.

VII. MARINE CONVENTIONS

321. A number of international conventions concerned with the control of marine pollution have been signed by the United Kingdom. These have been described in Chapter 4. The United Kingdom is playing an active part in the work of the Third United Nations Law of the Sea conference referred to in that chapter.

VIII. COUNCIL OF EUROPE

322. In general the Council of Europe no longer concerns itself directly with matters concerning environmental pollution though it continues to have a major interest in conservation and management of the natural environment.

RESPONSIBILITIES OF GOVERNMENT DEPARTMENTS IN ENVIRONMENTAL POLLUTION MATTERS

The following summary lists the principal responsibilities in the field of environmental pollution which are exercised by the various Government Departments and agencies. It does not cover those of their responsibilities with no bearing on environmental pollution. Except insofar as responsibility lies with the Scottish and Welsh Offices (see Sections 13 and 14 below) responsibilities here described are exercised throughout Great Britain.

It should be borne in mind that the first responsibility for many types of pollution control rests with water authorities or local authorities, as reference to the appropriate chapters above will make clear.

1. CABINET OFFICE

Normal Government machinery at Ministerial and Official levels for inter-departmental decisions on environmental matters.

2. DEPARTMENT OF THE ENVIRONMENT AND DEPARTMENT OF TRANSPORT

Co-ordination (through the Central Unit on Environmental Pollution) of central Government work on the control of pollution, clean air policy; control (with the Health and Safety Commission, through HM Alkali and Clean Air Inspectorate) of industrial emissions to the atmosphere; control (with the Health and Safety Commission) of dangerous goods in inland transport; control of pollution from traffic; policy on clearance of oil and hazardous substances from beaches; policy on disposal of waste, including toxic and radioactive wastes, and, in conjunction with Department of Industry, policy on waste management; policy on noise (except aircraft noise); policy and technical advice on water, sewerage and sewage disposal; physical planning policies and control; co-ordination of pollution research; co-ordination of environmental information and monitoring data exchange.

Research Establishments

(i) Transport and Road Research Laboratory: engaged on the assessment of the economic and social effects of environmental factors associated with transport, and methods of abating noise and pollution.

(ii) Building Research Establishment: concerned with the utilisation of waste materials and with noise in buildings.

(iii) Hydraulics Research Station: concerned with oil pollution control measures and with research into the causes of coastal erosion.

3. MINISTRY OF AGRICULTURE, FISHERIES AND FOOD

Protection of fisheries, including the control of dumping at sea; effects of environmental pollution on agriculture; pollution implications of agricultural practice, including the control of pesticides in agriculture and horticulture.

Research Establishments

(i) The Pest Infestation Control Laboratory and the Plant Pathology Laboratory: technical advice on pesticides.

(ii) The Agricultural Development and Advisory Service Regional Laboratories, Experimental Husbandry Farms, Experimental Horticultural Stations, the Farm Waste Unit and the Agricultural Research Council's Laboratories are all concerned with the management of farm wastes.

(iii) Fisheries Research Laboratories (Lowestoft and Burnham-on-Crouch), the Salmon and Freshwater Fisheries Laboratory: technical advice and monitoring of the effects of pollution on marine and freshwater life, including discharges of radioactive effluent into inland and coastal waters.

4. DEPARTMENT OF TRADE

Prevention of marine pollution; control of dangerous cargoes at sea; aircraft noise.

5. DEPARTMENT OF INDUSTRY

Industrial aspects of environmental pollution.

Research Establishments

(i) Warren Spring Laboratory: environmental pollution research, including air pollution, oil pollution of the sea, and municipal and industrial waste treatment and recovery.

(ii) Laboratory of the Government Chemist: analytical and advisory services to Government Departments, including environmental pollution. Research into methods of analytical chemistry in the environmental field. Operates the Pesticide Residue Analysis Information Service.

(iii) National Physical Laboratory: noise research, radiation standards.

6. DEPARTMENT OF HEALTH AND SOCIAL SECURITY

Medical aspects of environmental pollution.

7. DEPARTMENT OF ENERGY

Energy policy.
The Department is advised on the siting, safety and operation of nuclear power stations and plant by the Nuclear Installations Inspectorate, part of the Health and Safety Executive.

8. DEPARTMENT OF EMPLOYMENT

Responsibility for the health, safety and welfare of persons at work and for the protection of others against risks to health or safety in connection with the activities of persons at work. The general responsibility for these matters rests with the Health and Safety Commission.

9. HEALTH AND SAFETY COMMISSION

The Commission has general responsibility for securing the health, safety and welfare of persons at work and of other persons affected by work activity; for controlling the keeping and use of dangerous substances and for controlling emissions into the atmosphere from certain premises of noxious or offensive substances. Its operational arm, the Health and Safety Executive, includes the Alkali and Clean Air, Mines and Quarries, Factory, Nuclear Installations and Explosives Inspectorates and their laboratories at Cricklewood, Buxton and Sheffield.

10. DEPARTMENT OF EDUCATION AND SCIENCE

Funding of basic science principally through the Research Councils.

RESEARCH COUNCILS

(i)   The NATURAL ENVIRONMENT RESEARCH COUNCIL promotes and supports research in the environmental sciences.
(ii) The AGRICULTURAL RESEARCH COUNCIL promotes agricultural research, which includes the effects of pesticides.
(iii) The MEDICAL RESEARCH COUNCIL promotes medical research, including research into radiobiological effects.
(iv) The SCIENCE RESEARCH COUNCIL promotes some research in the environmental sciences.
(v)   The SOCIAL SCIENCE RESEARCH COUNCIL promotes some research into the social effects of environmental pollution.

11. FOREIGN AND COMMONWEALTH OFFICE

International implications of environmental policies.

12. MINISTRY OF DEFENCE

Supports research directly or partly related to air pollution.

13. SCOTTISH OFFICE

Within the Scottish Office, the Scottish Development Department has similar responsibilities to the Department of the Environment in respect of environmental protection, water, sewerage, waste disposal and air pollution; HM Industrial Pollution Inspectorate for Scotland controls air pollution from

86

registered works (on an agency basis for the Health and Safety Commission) and advises on the control of water pollution, the disposal of toxic wastes and the control of pollution arising from the use of radioactive substances; the Department of Agriculture and Fisheries for Scotland and the Scottish Home and Health Department have responsibilities in respect of agriculture, fisheries and health similar to those of MAFF and DHSS. DAFS also replaces DES as sponsor of ARC work for all work at ARC Institutes in Scotland.

14. WELSH OFFICE

Similar responsibilities to the Department of the Environment in respect of environmental protection, water, sewerage, waste disposal, air pollution and planning. Also responsibility for health and a shared responsibility for agriculture.

15. ROYAL COMMISSION ON ENVIRONMENTAL POLLUTION

The Royal Commission was established in 1970. Its terms of reference are to advise on matters, both national and international, concerning the pollution of the environment; on the adequacy of research in this field; and the future possibilities of danger to the environment.

Form of pollution	Government Department concerned	Controlling Directorate within Department or Executive body	Problem or area of responsibility
Air pollution	DOE	Noise, Clean Air and Coast Protection Division	Policy on smoke control and clean air.
		HSE (HM Alkali and Clean Air Inspectorate)	Air pollution from registered processes. Advice to local authorities on processes and operations outside the scope of the Alkali Acts.
	DTp	Directorate of Vehicle Engineering and Inspection	Emissions from motor vehicles.
	SDD	Water, Sewerage and Pollution Division	Policy on smoke control and clean air.
		HM Industrial Pollution Inspectorate for Scotland	Exercises similar functions to the Alkali Inspectorate on behalf of the Health and Safety Commission.
	WO	Environment Protection Unit	Policy on smoke control and clean air.
	WO	Environment Protection Unit and HSE	Air pollution from registered processes. Advice to local authorities on processes and operations outside the scope of the Alkali Acts.
		Local authorities	Control of domestic emissions and emissions from commercial and industrial processes outside the scope of the Alkali Inspectorate.
Freshwater pollution	DOE	Directorate of Water	Policy on water management.
	DOE	Directorate General of Water Engineering I, II and III (WE I–III)	Advice on the conservation and proper use of water resources, the provision of water supplies and sewerage facilities, the treatment and disposal of sewage and trade effluents and the protection of health and the quality of water.
	SDD	Engineering Division	
	SDD	HM Industrial Pollution Inspectorate	Advice on the control of water pollution.

Freshwater pollution continued	WO	Local Government Division	Policy on water management.
	WO	Directorate of Engineering	Advice on the conservation and proper use of water resources, the provision of water supplies and sewerage facilities, the treatment and disposal of sewage and trade effluents and the protection of health and the quality of water.
	MAFF	Fisheries Division	Effect of river pollution on fish.
	DAFS	Fisheries Division	
		Regional Water Authorities (in England)	Management of all water services.
		Welsh National Water Development Authority (in Wales)	
		Local authorities (in Scotland)	Sewerage and sewage disposal.
		River Purification Boards on the Scottish mainland and local authorities on the islands	Promotion of cleanliness of waters.
Marine pollution	MAFF	Fisheries Division	Overall control of marine pollution and dumping at sea, in order to safeguard fishery interests.
	DAFS		
	DEn	Petroleum Production Inspectorate	Pollution from drilling operations.
	DT	Marine Division	Control of oil pollution at sea.
	DOE	Noise, Clean Air and Coast Protection Division	Policy on control of oil and chemicals on beaches.
	WO	Environment Protection Unit	Policy on control of oil and chemicals on beaches.

Form of pollution	Government Department concerned	Controlling Directorate within Department or Executive body	Problem or area of responsibility
Marine pollution continued		Local authorities	Dealing with oil pollution on beaches.
Waste	DOE	Waste Disposal Division	Policy on waste disposal.
	DOE	Waste Division (part of WE II)	Advice on methods of collection and disposal of solid and toxic wastes.
	SDD	HM Industrial Pollution Inspectorate	Advice on the disposal of toxic wastes.
	SDD	Engineering Division	Advice on methods of waste collection and disposal.
	WO	Environment Protection Unit	Policy on waste disposal.
	WO	Directorate of Engineering	Advice on methods of collection and disposal of solid and toxic wastes.
		Local authorities	Collection and disposal of waste.
Radioactivity	DEn	Atomic Energy Division	General responsibility for atomic energy policy; treatment and storage of radioactive waste.
	DEn	HSE (Nuclear Installations Inspectorate)	Safety of nuclear power plants, licensing and inspecting of some nuclear installations.
	MAFF	Fisheries Radiobiological Laboratory and Atomic Energy Branch	Advice on all aspects of radioactive discharges in relation to marine food and agricultural interests.
	DOE	Wastes Division	Policy on radioactive waste management.
	DOE	Radiochemical Inspectorate (part of WE II)	Disposal of radioactive wastes, radioactive discharges.
		HSE (Alkali Inspectorate)	Discharges to the atmosphere.

Form of pollution	Government Department concerned	Controlling Directorate within Department or Executive body	Problem or area of responsibility
Radioactivity continued	DTp	Dangerous Goods Division	Transport of radioactive materials.
	WO	HM Industrial Pollution Inspectorate	Control of pollution arising from the use of radioactive substances.
		Environment Protection Unit	Policy on radioactive waste management.
Pesticides	MAFF DAFS	Environmental pollution, pesticides and Infestation Control Division	Control of pesticides and advice on the disposal of farm wastes.
Noise	DOE	Noise, Clean Air and Coast Protection Division	Co-ordination of noise policy.
	SDD	Water, Sewerage and Pollution Division	Policy on noise.
	WO	Environment Protection Unit	Policy on noise.
	DTp	Directorate of Vehicle Engineering and Inspection	Control of traffic noise.
	DT	Civil Aviation Division	General responsibility for aircraft noise.
	DE	HSE (Factory Inspectorate)	Noise within workplaces.
		Local authorities	Control of neighbourhood noise.

ANNEX B

IMPLEMENTATION OF THE CONTROL OF POLLUTION ACT AS AT JULY 1976

ENGLAND AND WALES

1. Implementation of parts of the Control of Pollution Act 1974 that would require substantial expenditure have been deferred due to the current economic climate. Provisions in the Act which introduce only discretionary powers or which do not involve significant public expenditure have, however, been implemented and came into force on 1 January 1976 in England and Wales. This includes some sections of Parts I (Waste on Land) and II (Pollution of Water) and the whole of Parts III (Noise), IV (Pollution of the Atmosphere), V (Supplementary Provisions) and VI (Miscellaneous and General).

2. The provisions in Part I that have been brought into force are those which extend the powers of local authorities to reclaim waste and to produce heat and electricity. They will enable the Secretary of State to make regulations relating to waste of which it is particularly difficult or dangerous to dispose: this power will be held in reserve for the time being.

3. As regards the main provisions of Part I, sections 3 to 11 (which establish a licensing system for the disposal of controlled waste) were brought into effect in England and Wales on 14 June 1976. It will not unfortunately be possible for the time being to make resources available for the survey and plan provided for in section 2, but local authorities who are in a position to do so are encouraged to go ahead with the survey and the plan in advance of the statutory provisions. All authorities should have regard to the need for adequate facilities for all the waste that requires to be disposed of in their areas, including that generated by industry, and to operate the new system with this in mind.

4. The sections of Part II that have been implemented are minor provisions relating to deposits and vegetation in rivers and the investigation of water pollution problems arising from abandoned mines. Sections which bring under control those discharges of trade effluent to the sewers previously exempted have also been brought into force. The implementation of the major provisions of Part II of the Act would place water authorities in a position where they would have to incur substantial capital expenditure, at a time when they are operating under increasingly severe capital investment restrictions and when they are under great public pressure to keep their charges as low as possible. Industry, which would be similarly affected, is also under severe economic pressure. In these circumstances the Government has reluctantly come to the conclusion that implementation of these provisions should be delayed. However, it attaches particular importance to making the administration of pollution control as open as possible; and water authorities and industry are being

encouraged to make more information available to the public. The position will be kept under constant review, with a view to implementing the whole of Part II of the Act as soon as the circumstances are judged to be right.

5. Regulations on appeals in relation to the noise provisions of the Act and an Order approving the British Standard Code of Practice on construction site noise for the purposes of Part III (Noise) have been laid. Regulations on the measurement and registration for the purposes of Part III (Noise) have also been laid, as have regulations on the measurement and registration of noise abatement zones.

6. Part IV of the Act contains provisions for reducing atmospheric pollution and enabling local authorities to collect and publish information about such pollution. Most of this part of the Act will not be fully effective until regulations are made later, but minor provisions which came into effect on 1 January 1976 include section 78, which clarifies the law on air pollution from cable burning, and certain amendments and repeals to clean air legislation.

7. The provisions in Parts V (Supplementary Provisions) and VI (Miscellaneous and General) which are being brought into force relate to the powers of local authorities to obtain information and to enter and to inspect premises; and to various amendments of enactments and repeals. Schedule 2 increases the penalties for a wide range of pollution offences.

SCOTLAND

8. The programme bringing provisions of the Act into effect in Scotland is being separately considered. A number of provisions in Parts I, III, IV, V and VI are already in force.

ANNEX C

ABBREVIATIONS USED IN THIS PUBLICATION

AERE	Atomic Energy Research Establishment
ARC	Agricultural Research Council
BNFL	British Nuclear Fuels Limited
BRE	Building Research Establishment
CAA	Civil Aviation Authority
CCMS	Committee on the Challenges of Modern Society
CEGB	Central Electricity Generating Board
CRISTAL	Contract Regarding an Interim Supplement to Tanker Liability for Oil Pollution
CUEP	Central Unit on Environmental Pollution (DOE)
DAFS	Department of Agriculture and Fisheries for Scotland
DE	Department of Employment
DEn	Department of Energy
DESCNET	Data Network on Environmentally Significant Chemicals
DHS	Department of Health for Scotland (now part of SHHD)
DHSS	Department of Health and Social Security
DOE	Department of the Environment
DI	Department of Industry
DT	Department of Trade
DTp	Department of Transport
ECDIN	European Chemical Data and Information Network
ECE	Economic Commission for Europe
EEC	European Economic Community
FRL	Fisheries Radiobiological Laboratory
GEMS	Global Environment Monitoring System
HMIPI	Her Majesty's Industrial Pollution Inspectorate for Scotland
HRS	Hydraulics Research Station
HSE	Health and Safety Executive
ICES	International Council for the Exploration of the Sea
ICRP	International Commission on Radiological Protection
IMCO	Inter-Governmental Maritime Consultative Organisation
IRPTC	International Register of Potentially Toxic Chemicals
IRS	International Referral Service for Sources of Environmental Information
MAFF	Ministry of Agriculture, Fisheries and Food
MARC	Monitoring and Assessment Research Centre
MHLG	Ministry of Housing and Local Government (now within DOE)
MRC	Medical Research Council
NATO	North Atlantic Treaty Organisation
NERC	Natural Environment Research Council

NCC	Nature Conservancy Council
NII	Nuclear Installations Inspectorate
NRPB	National Radiological Protection Board
NRS	National Referral System
OECD	Organisation for Economic Co-operation and Development
OPOL	Off-shore Pollution Liability Agreement
PCB	Polychloride Biphenyl
PIRC	Protection against Ionising Radiation Committee
PSPS	Pesticides Safety Precautions Scheme
SDD	Scottish Development Department
SHD	Scottish Home Department (now part of SHHD)
SHHD	Scottish Home and Health Department
SRC	Science Research Council
SSRC	Social Science Research Council
STACWQ	Standing Technical Advisory Committee on Water Quality
TOVALOP	Tanker Owners Voluntary Agreement Concerning Liability for Oil Pollution
TRRL	Transport and Road Research Laboratory
UKAEA	United Kingdom Atomic Energy Authority
UNEP	United Nations Environment Programme
VCM	Vinyl Chloride Monomer
WO	Welsh Office
WRC	Water Research Centre
WSL	Warren Spring Laboratory

BIBLIOGRAPHY

1. General

CONTROL OF POLLUTION ACT, 1974, Chapter 40, 144 pp; HMSO, 1974 (ISBN 010 544074 4)

DEPARTMENT OF THE ENVIRONMENT: Central Unit on Environmental Pollution. The monitoring of the environment in the United Kingdom (Pollution Paper No. 1) viii+66 pp; HMSO, 1974 (ISBN 011 750719 9)

DEPARTMENT OF THE ENVIRONMENT: Central Unit on Environmental Pollution. Lead in the environment and its significance to man, a report of an interdepartmental working party on heavy metals (Pollution Paper No. 2) (Chairman: J. A. Jukes) viii+47 pp; HMSO, 1974 (ISBN 011 750730 X)

DEPARTMENT OF THE ENVIRONMENT: Central Unit on Environmental Pollution. Controlling pollution: a review of Government action related to recommendations by the Royal Commission on Environmental Pollution (Pollution Paper No. 4) 40 pp; HMSO, 1975 (ISBN 011 750899 3)

DEPARTMENT OF THE ENVIRONMENT: Central Unit on Environmental Pollution. Chlorofluorocarbons and their effect on stratospheric ozone (Pollution Paper No. 5) v+71 pp; HMSO, 1976 (ISBN 011 751021 1)

ENVIRONMENTAL POLLUTION, ROYAL COMMISSION ON. First report. Cmnd 4585 [Chairman: Sir Eric Ashby] 60 pp; HMSO, 1971 (ISBN 10 145850 9)

ENVIRONMENTAL POLLUTION, ROYAL COMMISSION ON. Second report: three issues in industrial pollution. Cmnd 4894 [Chairman: Sir Eric Ashby] v+9 pp; HMSO, 1972 (ISBN 10 148940 4)

ENVIRONMENTAL POLLUTION, ROYAL COMMISSION ON. Third report: pollution in some British estuaries and coastal waters. Cmnd 5054 [Chairman: Sir Eric Ashby] vi+128 pp; HMSO, 1972 (ISBN 10 150540 X)

ENVIRONMENTAL POLLUTION, ROYAL COMMISSION ON. Fourth report: pollution control; progress and problems. Cmnd 5780 [Chairman: Sir Brian Flowers] v+98 pp; HMSO, 1974 (ISBN 0 10 157800 8)

ENVIRONMENTAL POLLUTION, ROYAL COMMISSION ON. Fifth report: air pollution control: an integrated approach. Cmnd 6371 [Chairman: Sir Brian Flowers] viii+130 pp; HMSO, 1976 (ISBN 0 10 163710 1)

MINISTRY OF HOUSING AND LOCAL GOVERNMENT. Protection of the environment. The fight against pollution. Cmnd 4373. 32 pp; HMSO, 1970 (ISBN 10 143730 7)

DEPARTMENT OF THE ENVIRONMENT: Library. Index of current government and government-supported research in environmental pollution in Great Britain, 1973–. 206 pp; The Department, 1974

DEPARTMENT OF THE ENVIRONMENT: Library. Register of Research 1975. Part IV, Environmental Pollution. v+258 pp; The Department, 1975 (ISBN 0 903197 49 9)

2. Air Pollution

DEPARTMENT OF THE ENVIRONMENT. Clean air today. vi+38 pp; HMSO, 1974 (ISBN 011 750718 0)

DEPARTMENT OF THE ENVIRONMENT. Annual reports on alkali etc works nos 107–111, 1970–1974. Presented by the Chief Inspectors. HMSO, 1971–1975
Issued jointly with the Scottish Development Department and the Welsh Office

DEPARTMENT OF THE ENVIRONMENT: Working Party on the Suppression of Odours from Offensive and Selected Other Trades.
Odours; report. Part 1. Assessment of the problem in Great Britain. [Chairman: F. H. H. Valentin] xiii+166 pp; Stevenage: Warren Spring Laboratory, 1974 (ISBN 856240 36 2)
Part 2. Best present practice in odour prevention and abatement. [Chairman: F. H. H. Valentin] xiv+227 pp; Stevenage: Warren Spring Laboratory, 1975 (ISBN 0 856240 47 8)

MINISTRY OF HOUSING AND LOCAL GOVERNMENT: Working Party on Grit and Dust Emissions. Report of the Working Party on Grit and Dust Emissions. [Chairman: Mr D. Hicks] 27 pp; HMSO, 1967 (SO Code No. 75-167)

DEPARTMENT OF THE ENVIRONMENT: Working Party on Grit and Dust Emissions. Report of the second Working Party. [Chairman: G. G. Thurlow] vii+30 pp; HMSO, 1974 (ISBN 0 11 750848 9)

CLEAN AIR COUNCIL. Information about industrial emissions to the atmosphere; report by a working party of the Council. [Chairman: Rear Admiral P. G. Sharp] 35 pp; HMSO, 1973 (ISBN 0 11 750632 X)

CENTRAL OFFICE OF INFORMATION. Towards cleaner air, a review of Britain's achievements; consulting editors Cremer and Warner. 34 pp; HMSO, 1973 (ISBN 11 750518 8)
Prepared by the Central Office of Information for the Department of the Environment and the British Overseas Board

WARREN SPRING LABORATORY. National survey on air pollution 1961–1971. 3 vols; HMSO, 1972–73

Vol. 1. General introduction; United Kingdom—a summary; South-East Region (exclusive London); Greater London Area. 196 pp; HMSO, 1972 (ISBN 11 410149 3)

Vol. 2. South-West Region; Wales Region; North-West Region. 208 pp; HMSO, 1973 (ISBN 11 410150 7)

Vol. 3. East Anglia, East Midlands and West Midlands. 108 pp; HMSO, 1973 (ISBN 11 410151 5)

ENVIRONMENTAL POLLUTION, ROYAL COMMISSION ON. Fifth report; Air pollution control: an integrated approach. Cmnd 6371. [Chairman: Sir Brian Flowers] viii+130 pp; HMSO, 1976 (ISBN 0 10 163710 1)

3. Freshwater Pollution

MINISTRY OF HOUSING AND LOCAL GOVERNMENT: Working Party on Sewage Disposal. Taken for Granted. Report of the Working Party on Sewage Disposal. [Chairman: Lena Jeger] vii+65 pp; HMSO, 1970 (ISBN 11 750220 0)
Joint publication with the Welsh Office

DEPARTMENT OF THE ENVIRONMENT. Report of a River Pollution Survey of England and Wales. 3 vols, HMSO, 1971–74
Vol. 1. Report 52 pp, 1971 (ISBN 11 750 454 8)
Vol. 2. Discharges and forecasts of improvement 248 pp; 1972 (ISBN 117 50 472 6)
Vol. 3. Discharges of sewage and industrial effluents to estuaries and coastal waters excluded from Volume 2 of the 1970 survey; and a summary of all effluent recorded in the survey and to other coastal waters. xii+32 pp; 1974 (ISBN 0 11 750 843 8)

DEPARTMENT OF THE ENVIRONMENT. River pollution survey of England and Wales. Updated 1972. River quality. vi+16 pp; HMSO, 1972 (ISBN 11 750 527 7)
Issued jointly with the Welsh Office

DEPARTMENT OF THE ENVIRONMENT. River pollution survey of England and Wales. Updated 1973. River Quality and Discharges of Sewage and Industrial Effluents. ix+62 pp; HMSO, 1975 (ISBN 0 11 750912 4)
Issued jointly with the Welsh Office

DEPARTMENT OF THE ENVIRONMENT. Report of a survey of the discharges of foul sewage to the coastal waters of England and Wales. x+20 pp; HMSO, 1973 (ISBN 11 750618 4)
Issued jointly with the Welsh Office

ENVIRONMENTAL POLLUTION, ROYAL COMMISSION ON. Pollution in four industrial estuaries, studies in relation to changes in population and industrial development; four case studies undertaken for the Royal Commission on Environmental Pollution; by Elizabeth Porter. x+98 pp; HMSO, 1973 (ISBN 11 730051 9)

DEPARTMENT OF THE ENVIRONMENT: Central Advisory Water Committee. The future management of water in England and Wales. [Chairman: Sir Alan Wilson]. ix+107 pp; HMSO, 1971 (ISBN 11 750396 7)

DEPARTMENT OF THE ENVIRONMENT. Background to water re-organisation in England and Wales. 40 pp; HMSO, 1973 (ISBN 11 750570 6)

WATER POLLUTION RESEARCH LABORATORY. [Annual] report of the Water Pollution Research Laboratory Steering Committee with the report of the Director of Water Pollution Research 1970. HMSO, 1971

WATER POLLUTION RESEARCH LABORATORY. Notes on water pollution 1971, No. 52 March. 1974, No. 64, March. Stevenage: The Laboratory, 1971–1974

Quarterly. Each of this series of leaflets contains notes on some aspects of the control of pollution

WATER RESEARCH CENTRE. Annual report, nineteenth, for the 15 months ended 31 March, 1974. Marlow, Bucks: The Centre, 1974

MINISTRY OF HOUSING AND LOCAL GOVERNMENT: Central Advisory Water Committee: Trade Effluents Sub-Committee. Final report. iv+52 pp; HMSO, 1960 (75-58-1)

DEPARTMENT OF THE ENVIRONMENT: Standing Technical Committee on Synthetic Detergents. 14th Progress Report. 38 pp; HMSO, 1973 (ISBN 11 750620 6)

 MINISTRY OF HOUSING AND LOCAL GOVERNMENT. Standards of effluents to rivers with particular reference to industrial effluents. 24 pp; HMSO, 1968 (ISBN 11 750048 8)

MINISTRY OF AGRICULTURE, FISHERIES AND FOODS. Farm waste disposal short-term leaflet No. 67. 24 pp; MAFF, 1973

SCOTTISH DEVELOPMENT DEPARTMENT. Towards cleaner water, rivers pollution survey of Scotland. ix+37 pp; Edinburgh: HMSO, 1972 (ISBN 11 490780)

4. Marine Pollution

WARREN SPRING LABORATORY. Oil pollution of the sea and shore; a study of remedial measures. [By J. Wardley Smith, OBE]. v+33 pp; HMSO, 1972 (11 410157 4)

MINISTRY OF TRANSPORT: Committee on prevention of pollution of the sea by oil. Report. v+50 pp; HMSO, 1953

DEPARTMENT OF TRADE. Manual on the Avoidance of Pollution of the sea by oil. 4th ed. 28 pp; HMSO, 1974 (ISBN 011 511155 7)

HOME OFFICE. The Torrey Canyon. Cmnd 3246. 12 pp; HMSO, 1967

HOUSE OF COMMONS: Select Committee on Science and Technology Coastal pollution. Report from the Select Committee on Science and Technology. Session 1967–68, HC 421. 55 pp; HMSO, 1968 (ISBN 10 242168 4)

HOUSE OF COMMONS: Select Committee on Science and Technology. Coastal pollution: Report, minutes of evidence, appendices and index. Session 1967–68, HC 421-I. 452 pp; HMSO, 1968 (ISBN 10 279768 4)

HOME OFFICE. Observations on the Report of the Select Committee on Science and Technology. Coastal Pollution. Cmnd 3880. 24 pp; HMSO, 1969 (ISBN 10 138800 4)

5. Waste Disposal

MINISTRY OF HOUSING AND LOCAL GOVERNMENT: Working Party on Refuse Collection. Refuse storage and collection; report of the Working Party on Refuse Collection. [Chairman: H. H. Browne]. vi+165 pp; HMSO, 1967 (75–184)

MINISTRY OF HOUSING AND LOCAL GOVERNMENT: Technical Committee on the Disposal of Solid Toxic Wastes. Report of the Technical Committee. [Chairman: Dr A. Key]. 106 pp; HMSO, 1970 (ISBN 11 75027 82) Issued jointly with the Scottish Development Department

DEPARTMENT OF THE ENVIRONMENT: Working Party on Refuse Disposal. Refuse Disposal: report of the Working Party. [Chairman: J. Sumner]. vi+199 pp; HMSO, 1971 (ISBN 11 750348 7)

DEPARTMENT OF THE ENVIRONMENT: Standing Committee on Research into Refuse Collection, Storage and Disposal. First Report. 24 pp; HMSO, 1973 (ISBN 11 750621 4)

DEPARTMENT OF THE ENVIRONMENT: Working Group on the Disposal of Awkward Household wastes; Report. [Chairman: J. Sumner]. v+42 pp; HMSO, 1974 (ISBN 0 11 750729 6)

DEPARTMENT OF THE ENVIRONMENT. War on waste. Policy for reclamation. Cmnd 5727. 33 pp; HMSO, 1974 (ISBN 0 10 157270 0) Issued jointly with the Department of Industry. A Green Paper

DEPARTMENT OF THE ENVIRONMENT. Library. Occasional Paper [No. 5]. Waste management research. iii+65 pp; The Department, 1975

DEPARTMENT OF THE ENVIRONMENT. Waste Management Advisory Council, 1st Report. iii+51 pp; HMSO, 1976 (ISBN 0 11 751007 6) Issued jointly with the Department of Industry

6. **Radioactivity**

MINISTRY OF HOUSING AND LOCAL GOVERNMENT. Control of radioactive wastes. Cmnd 884. 46 pp; HMSO, 1959

RADIOACTIVE SUBSTANCES ACT 1960. Chapter 34. 28 pp; HMSO, 1960

RADIOACTIVE SUBSTANCES, EXEMPTION ORDERS

S.I. 1962/2641	Civil Defence
1962/2643	Testing Instruments
1962/2644	Luminous Articles
1962/2645	Exhibitions
1962/2646	Storage in Transit
1962/2648	Phosphatic Substances, Rare Earths, etc
1962/2649	Lead
1962/2710	Uranium and Thorium
1962/2711	Prepared Uranium and Thorium Compounds
1962/2712	Geological Specimens
1962/2761	Luminous Articles (S)
1962/2762	Lead (S)
1962/2764	Testing Instruments (S)
1962/2765	Storage in Transit (S)
1962/2766	Uranium and Thorium (S)
1962/2767	Civil Defence (S)
1962/2768	Exhibitions (S)
1962/2769	Phosphatic Substances, Rare Earths, etc (S)
1962/2771	Geological Specimens (S)
1962/2772	Prepared Uranium and Thorium Compounds (S)
1963/1832	Schools etc
1963/1834	Thorium-X
1963/1835	Attachments to Lightning Conductors
1963/1836	Precipitated Phosphate
1963/1878	Schools etc (S)
1963/1880	Thorium-X (S)
1963/1881	Attachments to Lightning Conductors (S)
1963/1882	Precipitated Phosphate (S)
1967/1796	Fire Detectors
1967/1797	Electronic Valves
1967/1803	Electronic Valves (S)
1967/1804	Fire Detectors (S)
1968/935	Tokens for Vending Machines
1968/936	Vouchers for Encashment Machines
1968/953	Vouchers for Encashment Machines (S)
1968/954	Tokens for Vending Machines (S)

INTERNATIONAL COMMISSION ON RADIOLOGICAL PROTECTION: Committee 4 on the Application of Recommendations: Task Group on Environmental Monitoring. Principles of environmental monitoring related to the handling of radioactive materials; a report adopted by the Commission on 13 September 1965. (ICRP Publication 7) iv+11 pp; Pergamon Press, 1966

MEDICAL RESEARCH COUNCIL. The hazards to man of nuclear and allied radiations. Second report. Cmnd 1225. viii+154 pp; HMSO, 1960

DEPARTMENT OF THE ENVIRONMENT. Code of practice for the carriage of radio-active materials by road. 92 pp; HMSO, 1975 (ISBN 0 11 550348 X)

7. Pesticides

DEPARTMENT OF THE ENVIRONMENT: Central Unit on Environmental Pollution. The non-agricultural uses of pesticides in Great Britain; a report. (Pollution Paper No. 3). vi+65 pp; HMSO, 1974 (ISBN 0 11 750849 7)

DEPARTMENT OF EDUCATION AND SCIENCE: Advisory Committee on Pesticides and other Toxic Chemicals. Further review of certain persistent organochlorine pesticides used in Great Britain; report by the Advisory Committee. iii+148 pp; HMSO, 1969 (ISBN 11 270152 3)

ORGANISATION FOR ECONOMIC CO-OPERATION AND DEVELOPMENT: Study Group on Unintended Occurrence of Pesticides. The problems of persistent chemicals; implications of pesticides and other chemicals in the environment. 113 pp; Paris: OECD, 1971

MINISTRY OF AGRICULTURE, FISHERIES AND FOOD: Agricultural Chemicals Approval Scheme. [Annual] List of approved products and their uses for farmers and growers. 1975. 183 pp; MAFF, 1975

8. Noise

NOISE ADVISORY COUNCIL. Aircraft noise; flight routeing near airports, report by a working group of the Council. [Chairman: E. Epson]. 37 pp; HMSO, 1971 (ISBN 11 750416 5)

NOISE ADVISORY COUNCIL. Neighbourhood noise; report by the working group on the Noise Abatement Act. [Chairman: Sir Hilary Scott]. vii+81 pp; HMSO, 1971 (ISBN 11 750453 X)

NOISE ADVISORY COUNCIL. Aircraft noise: should the Noise and Number Index be revised? Report by the Research Sub-Committee of the Council. 6 pp; HMSO, 1972 (ISBN 11 750519 6)

NOISE ADVISORY COUNCIL. Traffic noise, the vehicle regulations and their enforcement; report by a working group of the Council. [Chairman: D. B. Harrison]. vi+67 pp; HMSO, 1972 (ISBN 11 750478 5)

DEPARTMENT OF THE ENVIRONMENT. A guide to noise units; [prepared by] the Noise Advisory Council. 8 pp; The Department, 1974

NOISE ADVISORY COUNCIL. Noise in the next ten years; report by the Panel on Noise in the Seventies. [Chairman: Professor E. J. Richards]. vii+15 pp; HMSO, 1974 (ISBN 0 11 750716 4)

NOISE ADVISORY COUNCIL. Aircraft engine noise research, report by the Research Sub-Committee at the Council. [Chairman: Dr H. P. Stout]. 15 pp; HMSO, 1974 (ISBN 0 11 750717 2)

NOISE ADVISORY COUNCIL. Aircraft noise: review of aircraft departure routeing policy; report by a working group of the Council. [Chairman: Eric Epson]. vi+29 pp; HMSO, 1974 (ISBN 0 11 750 735 0)

NOISE ADVISORY COUNCIL. Noise in public places; report by a working group of the Council. [Chairman: H. Archer]. v+32 pp; HMSO, 1974 (ISBN 0 11 750736 9)

NOISE ADVISORY COUNCIL. Noise units; report by a Working Party for the Research Sub-Committee of the Council. 17 pp; HMSO, 1975 (ISBN 0 11 750864 0)

NOISE ADVISORY COUNCIL. Bothered by noise? How the law can help you. 12 pp; The Council, 1975

DEPARTMENT OF THE ENVIRONMENT. Land compensation—your rights explained. 2. Your home and nuisance from public development. 12 pp; The Department, 1973
Prepared jointly with the Welsh Office and the Central Office

DEPARTMENT OF THE ENVIRONMENT. Land compensation—your rights explained. 5. Insulation against traffic noise. 13 pp; HMSO, 1975

DEPARTMENT OF THE ENVIRONMENT. Structure and local plans—your opportunity. 3 pp; HMSO, 1973
Prepared jointly with the Welsh Office and the Central Office of Information

DEPARTMENT OF THE ENVIRONMENT. Public inquiries into road proposals; what you will need to know. i+18 pp; The Department, 1973

DEPARTMENT OF THE ENVIRONMENT. Calculation of road traffic noise. 94 pp; HMSO, 1975 (ISBN 0 11 550 367 6)
Joint publication with the Welsh Office

OFFICE OF POPULATION CENSUSES AND SURVEYS: Social Survey Division. Second survey of aircraft noise annoyance around London (Heathrow) Airport. 200 pp; HMSO, 1971 (ISBN 11 70047 7)
Prepared by M. I. L. Research Ltd for the Social Survey Division on behalf of the Department of Trade and Industry

OFFICE OF THE MINISTER FOR SCIENCE: Committee on the Problem of Noise. Final report. [Chairman: Sir Alan Wilson]. Cmnd 2056. HMSO, 1963

DEPARTMENT OF TRADE AND INDUSTRY. Action against aircraft noise; progress report 1973. 22 pp; The Department, 1973
Prepared jointly with the Central Office of Information

DEPARTMENT OF EMPLOYMENT. Code of practice for reducing the exposure of employed persons to noise. 32 pp; HMSO, 1972 (11 360 887 X)

BRITISH STANDARDS INSTITUTION. Code of practice for noise control on construction and demolition sites. (ES 5228: 1975). 35 pp; BSI, 1975 (ISBN 0 580 08874 X)

DEPARTMENT OF EMPLOYMENT. Research 1972–73. HMSO, 1973–

9. International

ORGANISATION FOR ECONOMIC CO-OPERATION AND DEVELOPMENT. OECD at work for the environment. 57 pp; OECD, 1973

DECLARATION OF THE COUNCIL OF THE EUROPEAN COMMUNITIES on programme of action on the environment. (Official Journal of the European Communities, 1973, Vol. 16, No. C112, December, 53 pp)

Printed in England for Her Majesty's Stationery Office
by Staples Printers Limited
Dd 587465 K20 10/76